"I've learned more about pra[...] any writer, theologian, or pastor. Julia has spent her life praying for 'big things,' and the results have been miraculous. I know you will be encouraged, inspired, and, yes, entertained as you read Julia's story and discover the principles about effective praying that will transform your life."

Dr. Robert Jeffress, pastor of First Baptist Church, Dallas,
Bible teacher, and host of *Pathway to Victory*

"When we walk through tough times we can turn to despair that clouds our vision or prayer that clears our path. Julia shows us clearly how to pray big prayers to an even bigger God."

Sheila Walsh, author of *It's Okay Not to Be Okay*

"From the moment I began reading *Pray Big Things*, Julia's words challenged my faith in unexpected ways. Her presentation of biblical truth and her honesty in sharing her personal journey will inspire you to dream beyond what seems possible, to start praying big prayers, and, most importantly, to believe God is powerful enough to answer them!"

Debbie Lindell, lead pastor of James River Church, author of
She Believes, and host of the Designed for Life Conference

"With courage and compassion, Julia Jeffress Sadler shares her deeply personal journey of suffering and loss that would make anyone want to swallow back tears. But through her faith-filled words, we can discover how to boldly hang on to God's promises, pray big things, and experience heaven's blessings! If you're searching for hope in the darkness, this book is a must-read!"

Rachel Lamb Brown, Daystar Television Network

"Julia Jeffress Sadler is a walking testimony of the faithfulness of God to answer prayer. After three miscarriages in one year—then, after praying for triplets and giving birth only to learn that each of the three needed separate and different medications, she continued to believe God to do the impossible for her newborns. *Pray Big Things* by Julia Jeffress Sadler will definitely enlarge your concept of prayer, answer your questions about some of the mysteries of answered/unanswered prayer, and really get you excited about the potential of God's prayer promises being fulfilled—in *your* life! But only if you read it."

Marcus D. Lamb, founder and president
of Daystar Television Network

"You are not simply going to love this book but will profit from it greatly. Julia shares principles that she has personally beaten out on the anvil of her own personal experience. Order more than one copy now because you will want to give one to someone you know who needs these truths."

O. S. Hawkins, author of the bestselling Code series
of devotionals including *The Joshua Code*
and *The Jesus Code*

"Often, how we view God determines the size of our faith in Him. If we have a small view of God, we'll have a small faith. If we have a big view of God, we'll have a big faith. I am so thankful my friend Julia wrote this book, *Pray Big Things*. We can pray big prayers because we are praying to a big God! Read this book. Share this book."

Shane Pruitt, author of 9 *Common Lies Christians Believe*

"*Pray Big Things* is a beautiful story of God doing the impossible and answering Julia's bold prayers. It's filled with hope and encouragement and contains a challenge to view God through a much bigger lens. If you want to pray big things in your own life, this book is for you. We can't wait to see how God uses *Pray Big Things* in the lives of everyone who reads it."

Kristen Clark and **Bethany Beal**, cofounders
of GirlDefined Ministries and authors
of *Sex, Purity, and the Longings of a Girl's Heart*

PRAY BIG THINGS

The Surprising Life God Has for You
When You're BOLD ENOUGH TO ASK

JULIA JEFFRESS SADLER

BakerBooks
a division of Baker Publishing Group
Grand Rapids, Michigan

Published by Baker Books
a division of Baker Publishing Group
PO Box 6287, Grand Rapids, MI 49516-6287
www.bakerbooks.com

Printed in the United States of America

Library of Congress Cataloging-in-Publication Data
Names: Sadler, Julia Jeffress, 1988– author.
Title: Pray big things : the surprising life God has for you when you're bold enough to ask / Julia Jeffress Sadler, MA, LPC.
Description: Grand Rapids : Baker Books, a division of Baker Publishing Group, 2019. | Includes bibliographical references.
Identifiers: LCCN 2019002825 | ISBN 9780801093364 (pbk.)
Subjects: LCSH: Prayer—Christianity.
Classification: LCC BV210.3 .S235 2019 | DDC 248.3/2—dc23
LC record available at https://lccn.loc.gov/2019002825

The author is represented by The Fedd Agency, Inc.

19 20 21 22 23 24 25   7 6 5 4 3 2 1

To Ryan, Blair, Barrett, and Blake,
who are immeasurably more than anything
I could have hoped or imagined!
God put you in my heart, dreams, and prayers
long before He put you in my life.

May this book help you to forever remember our story,
remember our God, and remember to pray big things!

Let the redeemed of the LORD tell their story—
those he redeemed from the hand of the foe.
Psalm 107:2 NIV

Contents

Acknowledgments

As I strive to write my dedication and acknowledgment pages between my triplets' nap times, I am amazed by how much has happened in the past two years. Putting the final touches on my first book while balancing three one-year-olds is a predicament I could have only dreamed of a few years ago. I was broken, I was exhausted, and I was being spiritually attacked, but I kept hearing God tell me *Just keep going*, and eventually my mantra, challenge, and vision changed to *Pray big things*!

I probably shouldn't give any spoilers, so I'll just leave it at this: a first-time mom of triplets cannot write a book while taking care of three babies without a ton of help! *Pray Big Things* is the culmination of a lot of prayer, people, support, and God's power. It's a story and charge that I believe God wants told and applied, and because of that, He called me and at times carried me through the process to get His promises to you!

My biggest thank-you goes to God for allowing me to walk this path and come out smiling and sharing on the other side. He prepared me, called me, carried me, comforted me, and inspired me. Jesus gave me His dreams for my life and allowed me to take part in a two-year battle that left me and thousands of others praising Him. To God be the glory!

My second biggest thank-you is to my husband, Ryan. This book would not have happened without him. Ryan, when I think about your influence on this book I think of three things: (1) You agreeing to "shifts" at night for the babies and allowing me to set a 2:00 a.m. alarm so I could get up and write. (2) You telling me years ago, when I was discouraged, "I think this is only the beginning of our story." (3) You sleeping next to me on the couch of the hospital for fifty days straight, refusing to leave my side. You're the real deal, Ryan, and I just hope to be in the same neighborhood as you in heaven!

Pray Big Things is the story we lived and one we realized needed to be shared with as many people as possible. Hope is contagious. I was so blessed to have others who caught the same vision and helped make my dream of this book a reality.

Special thanks to:

Brian Vos and the entire team at Baker Publishing Group for taking a chance on a first-time author who managed to get pregnant with triplets in the middle of a book manuscript deadline! I will forever be grateful for your expertise, grace, excitement, wisdom, and belief in me!

Whitney Gossett and the entire team at The Fedd Agency for your tireless hours, enthusiastic spirit, and hard work on this project. You are a joy to work with!

Jennifer Stair for your literary expertise and helping me cross the finish line!

Brittany Hamilton for your incredible gift of designing and editing that is pure art and makes my ideas a reality.

My friends and family who encouraged, helped, inspired, and believed in me every step of the way, especially Ambree Christy, Lindsey Curtis, Nate Curtis, Ginny Lauren Hulette, Dorothy Jeffress, Megan Harney, Shane Pruitt, Janae Gibson, and Melody Allen.

The thousands who prayed for our babies, shared in our tears and joys, told us their stories, and entrusted us with their prayers. We felt the army behind and before us, and we continually thank the Lord for you!

My parents, Robert and Amy Jeffress, for leading the way in sharing the good news of the gospel through writing and speaking! Your incredible legacy of faith, unwavering commitment to God's Word, and hearts for evangelism will continue to impact generations to come in our family and in our world.

My "Confetti Club" for encouraging me every step of the way. Parris, Kelley, Vanessa, Paige, Erin, Joni, Ana, Emily, and Shea, I truly believe your celebration of these little lives was the morale boost I needed to survive!

First Baptist Dallas members, staff, and students, I am convinced you are the best church and student ministry in the world! Thank you for being our prayer warriors and for being our family.

Blair, Barrett, and Blake, you were dreamed of, prayed for, and loved more than you will ever know! Your story is an encouragement to the discouraged and an incredible victory for God's team. Thank you for being the biggest blessings and the best story of our lives!

Introduction

Pray Big Things

N o one prays for triplets," a mom posted in my newly joined Facebook support group for parents of triplets, which has a screening process equivalent to being rushed for a sorority, followed by membership instructions that rival *Mission Impossible*. No use searching for us on Facebook; our group cannot be found unless someone adds you to the secret society.

"We prayed for triplets!" I remember proudly, humbly, and excitedly typing back. Why do I say *proudly*? Doesn't that contradict *humbly*? Nope. My husband, Ryan, and I are so proud of God and of what He has done to redeem our losses and give us more than we could ever imagine that we want to shout it from the rooftops. God sustained us through multiple miscarriages, losses, jealousy, bitterness, discouragement, suffering, and exhaustion, and He has blessed us now beyond our wildest imagination.

That's all good for you, you may be thinking, *but what does your story have to do with me? I've prayed before and haven't received what I've asked. And sometimes I don't even know what I would ask God if I could.*

What if I told you God wants to do more than you can possibly imagine in your life? First Corinthians 2:9 declares, "No eye has seen, no ear has heard, and no mind has imagined what God has prepared for those who love him" (NLT). Your dream may not be to have triplets, but if you are honest with yourself, it is likely you have a dream deep down that you would give anything in order to make happen. My challenge to you is to start imagining what would happen if God fulfilled that dream!

> *What if I told you God wants to do more than you can possibly imagine in your life?*

After we miscarried three babies in one year, Ryan and I came to a point of desperation and made a decision that changed our lives forever: we committed to start praying for big things. As I will describe in more detail in the chapters to come, we prayed fervently for three biological children, prayed for multiples, prayed for miracles, prayed for a TV show, prayed for book deals, and prayed to have children of both genders. Nearly one year to the day of our last miscarriage, God answered our big prayers in a big way: by giving us triplets, a television show, and the opportunity to share our story through books.

These may not be your specific dreams, goals, or prayers, but they show that God is an active God who listens to our requests. The Bible says, "You don't have what you want because you don't ask God for it" (James 4:2 NLT). This verse has been the theme of our prayer journey. While God is not a genie in the sky granting whatever we wish for, the truth is that the majority of Christians today are not asking too much of God; they are asking too little of God.

So, what are you waiting for? Are you wondering why God isn't answering your prayers? Do you want more in your life? Do you want God to act? Do you have dreams that seem impossible? Are you tired of living in the future or the past? Do you wonder how to keep moving, keep loving, and keep acting in the midst of suffering, in the midst of questions, and in the midst of knowing and believing God is good while trying to come to terms with the place you find yourself in life? If you are tired of "wishing your life away" by wishing for things without actually taking any action and are ready to see God move in your life like never before, then this book is for you.

> *The majority of Christians today are not asking too much of God; they are asking too little of God.*

This is the story of our waiting, infertility, ceaseless praying, struggles, and ultimately receiving more than we could imagine. This is the story of pain, loss, hope, and dreams fulfilled. This story is for you, so that you do not lose heart, so that you will refuse to give up, and so that you will choose to believe God to be the powerful dream creator and prayer answerer He is. This is not a seminary-level book about the spiritual discipline of prayer. This is a book for ordinary people about the experiences of one ordinary family who decided to start taking God at His Word and seeing what would happen. Also, by looking at the life of the biblical character Joseph, we will see that God often gives us our dreams long before they come to fruition.

My prayer, as you read this book, is that you will leave encouraged, believing God can do immeasurably more than anything you can hope or imagine. May you begin with new excitement, courage, and determination to pray big things!

1

More Than We Can Imagine

Never measure God's unlimited power by your limited expectations.

David C. McCasland

I think we should get married," I said to my boyfriend, Ryan, when we were both fourteen years old and in junior high. "Our personalities seem really compatible."

This was a few months prior to the inevitable breakup that began a long romantic saga to rival every great teen drama and before my mom called Ryan to get him and me back together (every teenage boy's dream, right?). This was also before we got married at ages twenty and twenty-one, when everyone thought we were too young and too immature, and before we were both called to full-time student ministry. This was before we were the first to get married and the last to have kids in our friend group, before our three miscarriages—and before the miraculous birth of our triplets.

This was also before the journey that would test our faith, before Ryan and I truly believed God, and before we made a decision one rainy New Year's Eve night in London to pray big things.

This one decision to start praying intentionally—to ask God regularly for very specific requests—has changed the course of our lives forever. And it has the potential to change your life as well.

Living on Borrowed Prayers

For most of my life, I was never really interested in prayer. Prayer seemed boring, honestly.

I understand if reading that makes you decide I seem unspiritual. Maybe you think perhaps I was new to the Christian faith, and the reason I wasn't interested in prayer was that I hadn't been exposed to the spiritual discipline. But the truth is that I have been in church my entire life. As the daughter of a pastor, I was praying before bed and at the dinner table ever since I could talk. I have had a front-row seat to witnessing God's miraculous answers to the incredible prayers of His people since an early age. And now, as a full-time student minister married to another student minister, I have had the opportunity to watch God move in the lives of young people in astounding ways in response to their fervent prayers.

So why was prayer not exciting to me? Why did I secretly think it was boring and nod off while listening to sermons about it?

The answer is *I was living on borrowed prayers*.

I had benefited from other people's knee work. I had been encouraged by other people's testimonies. I had gotten chill bumps while listening to other people pray. But none of my experiences with prayer had been direct, personal encounters with God. My lack of enthusiasm about prayer was not a theological issue; it was an ownership issue. I lived and benefited from borrowed prayers for most of my life.

Let me stop and say that others interceding on our behalf is incredible, biblical, and very important to the Christian life. But it cannot be our only experience with prayer. If we want to see God move and do big things in our lives, then we must have a direct line to Him.

> *If we want to see God move and do big things in our lives, then we must have a direct line to Him.*

While the term "borrowed prayers" is not in the Bible, the theme of borrowing versus ownership can be found throughout Scripture. Ryan and I have worked in student ministry for the past ten years. A few years into our ministry, the Barna Group released a landmark study, based on a five-year project headed by David Kinnaman, which found that "nearly three out of every five young Christians (59%) disconnect either permanently or for an extended period of time from church life after age 15."[1] This was a knife to the hearts of Christian parents and student ministers who devote their lives to helping adolescents develop and maintain a strong Christian faith.

What needs to happen in order to keep our teenagers in church? How do we make sure that, after sending our students off to college, we are not also sending them off forever from the church? Ryan and I, along with many other student ministers, have realized that one of the reasons teenagers are leaving church is they have not developed authentic ownership over their faith. They may have a faith background, and they may be familiar with the things of God, but they haven't developed a personal faith of their own by seeking and believing in Him for themselves. Since their faith has been fueled only by the faith of their parents or church community, and not by God Himself, they are susceptible to burnout.

I think the same principle can be found with Christians of all ages. A lack of ownership equals a lack of enthusiasm, resulting in a susceptibility to abandoning our faith. When we don't take ownership of our faith, we are not excited about it, resulting many times in the temporary, practical, or permanent abandonment of our faith.

Maybe we don't abandon it altogether. Maybe we just decide to stop doing certain spiritual disciplines, like prayer, that do not seem to be working for us anymore. We slowly let other people do our knee work, and before we know it, we end up massively out of spiritual shape.

The Bible repeatedly refers to God's people taking ownership of the blessings God has promised to His children. For example, Deuteronomy 15:6 says, "The LORD your God will bless you as He has promised you, and you will lend to many nations, but you will not borrow; and you will rule over many nations, but they will not rule over you." Or consider Deuteronomy 28:12, which says, "The LORD will open for you His good storehouse, the heavens, to give rain to your land in its season and to bless all the work of your hand; and you shall lend to many nations, but you shall not borrow." While some things in these chapters are specific to the historic time period and to the Israelites, the idea that we are to own what God has promised and not be in a state of borrowing is a truth applicable to Christians today.

It is a complete contradiction for us to live as if we have no tangible way to get what we need, want, or desire while having full access to the God of all creation.

This does not mean it is always wrong to borrow things. For example, you can borrow sugar, a lawn mower, or another household need from your neighbor. Rather, these passages are saying that it is a complete contradiction for us to live as if we have no tangible way to get what we need, want, or desire while having full access to the God of all creation.

Your Greatest Adventure

This is not a theology book, and I am not a theologian. I do sometimes say I have an honorary degree from Pastor's Daughter Seminary, after years of having my bedtime story be my dad telling me the points of his upcoming sermon or a detailed explanation of the differences between various world religions. But you do not have to be a theologian to understand the Bible. You don't even need to have grown up in church. Faith is so simple that the Bible says even a child can understand (Matt. 18:3).

While there are countries in the world today where reading the Bible is illegal and punishable by the government, chances are, since you are reading this book, you probably don't live in one of these places. This means you are more

than likely allowed limitless access to the Bible. The Bible—
which defines, details, and declares supernatural truth and
reveals secrets to unleashing incredible power over our lives—
remains for many of us a dusty book, doubling as a coaster
on a bad day and as bookshelf decor on the best day. Why
do many Christians go days, weeks, months, or even years
without reading the text that defines their professed faith?

Someone has wisely said, "A person who won't read has
no advantage over one who can't read." The same principle
applies when it comes to the practice
of prayer. The person who won't pray
has no advantage over the person who
can't pray.

> *Many of God's children are not asking for much more than a blessed meal, resulting in a less-than-blessed life.*

Wait a minute, you may be thinking. *What do you mean "the person
who can't pray"? Can't everyone pray?*
Well, of course they can pray. But as
Christians, we have a special relation-
ship to the Father. The apostle Peter tells us that "the eyes
of the Lord are toward the righteous, and His ears attend to
their prayer" (1 Pet. 3:12). However, many of God's children
are not asking for much more than a blessed meal, resulting
in a less-than-blessed life.

Why Don't We Receive Answers to Our Prayers?

Contrary to popular social media posts and bumper stickers,
we are not all children of God. The Bible says in John 1:12,
"To all who did receive [Jesus], to those who believed in his
name, he gave the right to become children of God" (NIV).
Anyone who receives Christ as personal Lord and Savior is a

child of God and has unlimited access to ask whatever they wish of their heavenly Father.

We Are Not Children of God

Some of us are not receiving what we ask because we are not really children of God. If you have never received Christ as your personal Lord and Savior, then I urge you not to read another word of this book without asking God to forgive you and save you, and asking for Jesus's sacrifice on the cross to count for you. Romans 10:9–10 says, "If you confess with your mouth Jesus as Lord, and believe in your heart that God raised Him from the dead, you will be saved; for with the heart a person believes, resulting in righteousness, and with the mouth he confesses, resulting in salvation." If you are not yet a Christian (or not sure if you are), then I encourage you to stop right now and pray something like this:

Dear God,

Thank You for loving me. I realize that I have failed You in many ways, and I'm truly sorry for the sin in my life. I believe that You loved me so much that You sent Your Son Jesus to die on the cross for me. I believe that Jesus took the punishment from You that I deserve for my sins. So right now I'm trusting in what Jesus did for me—not my own good works—to save me from my sins. Thank You for forgiving me and helping me to spend the rest of my life serving You. In Jesus's name I pray. Amen.

If you prayed and just became a child of God, then welcome to the family! You have made the most important decision of your life. You can rest assured that you are sealed with the Holy Spirit and will spend eternity with Jesus in heaven. As the apostle John wrote, "These things I have written to you who believe in the name of the Son of God, so that you may know that you have eternal life" (1 John 5:13).

You also now have unlimited access to ask whatever you want, need, or desire of your heavenly Father, who loves, hears, and answers His children. In John 15:16, Jesus encourages believers, "You did not choose Me but I chose you, and appointed you that you would go and bear fruit, and that your fruit would remain, so that whatever you ask the Father in My name He may give to you." If you have accepted Christ as your personal Lord and Savior, then Jesus's Father is now your heavenly Father, of whom you can ask anything and everything.

We Are Not Living like Children of God

Some of us are not receiving what we ask in prayer because we are living as if we are not children of God. We are not asking anything of God, even though we can ask everything of Him!

UNCONFESSED SIN

We may not be interested in praying because of unconfessed sin in our lives. Sin creates a sense of estrangement from God. Isaiah 59:2 says, "Your iniquities have made a separation between you and your God, and your sins have hidden *His* face from you so that He does not hear." When we are living in sin, we tend to pull away from God and stop coming to Him in prayer.

King David knew what it was like for his sin to create a barrier between him and God. In Psalm 40:12–13, he wrote,

"Evils beyond number have surrounded me; my iniquities have overtaken me, so that I am not able to see; they are more numerous than the hairs of my head, and my heart has failed me. Be pleased, O LORD, to deliver me; make haste, O LORD, to help me."

DISAPPOINTMENT WITH UNANSWERED PRAYERS

We also may not be interested in praying because of prayers that were not answered in the past and resulted in disappointment and hurt. I remember trying to help a young woman in our eleventh-grade Sunday school class become excited about prayer during student ministry. She replied, "Julia, I want to pray, but it is hard to believe God will answer. You see, when I was a little girl, I begged God every night to take my mom's cancer away. But He did not heal her, and she died."

I cannot explain away heartbreaking circumstances in life. Some things that happen in our lives are too horrible, too sad, too discouraging, or too traumatic to try to understand this side of heaven. I firmly believe nothing happens to us that God has not ordained, and that He will sustain us through anything if we let Him. I do not fully understand why some prayer requests in my life and your life have not been answered in ways we wanted them to be answered. However, I do have faith in God's ability to sustain and encourage us through even the most terrible events in our lives and to use them to bring us closer to Him.

Romans 8:28 tells us, "We know that God causes all things to work together for good to those who love God, to those who are called according to His purpose." We can rest assured that when difficult circumstances come into our lives, God is still in control, and He has a purpose.

I remember clinging to this truth during all three of our miscarriages. I could not explain why they had happened. I could not find any nice pretty bow of purpose to put on the most devastating losses of our lives. All I could do was follow the wisdom of a former client who was trying to make sense of her father abandoning her family. She told me, "Julia, I decided either God is who He says He is, or He isn't. There really is no other decision to be made." I decided to believe God was in control and knew what He was doing with every lost pregnancy, every lost dream, and every temptation Satan put in my mind to doubt God's power and goodness.

> *We can rest assured that when difficult circumstances come into our lives, God is still in control, and He has a purpose.*

Someday We Will See God's Purpose

Probably the number-one thing I am most looking forward to about heaven is finally seeing behind the curtain. I am excited to see God's full purpose for all I experienced on earth—the good, the bad, the happy, and the painful. I can picture myself dying. (This is the morbid perspective you develop when you grow up having to plan your weekend activities around all the funerals your dad officiates on Saturdays; you end up thinking about death and funerals more than the average person.) And I imagine that when I get to heaven, God will pull out a massive map that connects all the dots of the events, people, choices, circumstances, prayer requests He said yes to, and prayer requests He said no to. I will look at God, smile, and say, "I get it now! Thank You."

Sometimes we get a sneak peek at how the dots are all connected, but I'm convinced the majority of our life maps will not be revealed this side of heaven. Our comfort does not depend on decoding our life map but on the knowledge, acceptance, and trust that there is, in fact, a carefully designed, colored, and marked map lovingly planned by our Creator. We are not the victims of random circumstances.

We want peace; we want understanding; we want to make sense of our lives. But, as C. S. Lewis said, "God cannot give us a happiness and peace apart from Himself, because it is not there. There is no such thing."[2]

We are adventurers who, though we encounter obstacles on our journeys, have been invited on a tailor-made quest to discover our unique purposes. This quest is marked with mountains, valleys, rivers, and giants, and it will be the adventure of our lifetime. This great adventure is reserved for the people who pray for big things.

The Night That Changed Everything

Our journey of praying big things began a few years ago on the New Year's Eve we spent in London, England. After attending an evening church service, Ryan and I went back to our hotel inspired but also skeptical. During the service, the pastor had led a guided prayer time and said, "Who in here wants God to bless their family?" People around us started yelling, clapping, and raising their hands. Ryan and I looked sheepishly at one another and exchanged an approving nod before raising our hands as well. Something about being on another continent made it easier for us to participate in the worship service of another Christian denomination that was very different from how we traditionally prayed and worshiped.

Ryan and I were not in a particularly desperate time in our lives. Neither of us was dying from a fatal illness or in need of miraculous physical healing. We weren't going bankrupt or in a financial crisis. We were just dreading another year of making wholehearted New Year's resolutions followed by little to no actual change. We were tired of promising, planning, and praying to live differently in the coming year, but by January 15—or maybe February if we *really* tried—ending up being the same people with the same marriage and the same circumstances and the same relationship with God.

So we got to planning and dreaming (as only two millennial Americans who find themselves in Europe inspired by a New Year's Eve prayer service can do). We started asking, What if? What if we really started taking God at His Word? What if we really believed God could and would answer our prayers? What if, instead of just saying, singing, and teaching that God answers prayers and is faithful, we actually started living like it? What if, by actually praying and pleading with God consistently, we allowed Him to work in our lives like never before?

That night, we decided, committed, promised, and planned to pray big things.

If We Only Knew . . .

I love everything about movies: going to the theater, the Academy Awards, seeing the newest hit film, imagining myself in the role of leading lady, and later trying to manufacture romantic moments with Ryan that are legendary Best Picture–worthy.

In these moments, Ryan usually is looking at me like I'm crazy and wondering what camera I'm talking to (think *The Truman Show*). You know when you are watching the scene that is going to change the course of the entire character's life, but the character doesn't know this yet. The audience winks at one another and bumps elbows as if to say, "Oh man, if these characters only knew what was about to happen, they would know that this night is about to change everything."

This is how I picture God, the angels, and my late grandmother, Judy Jeffress, talking among themselves as they watched Ryan and me this fateful night. I picture them smiling and nudging one another as they say something to the effect of, "Oh man, if Ryan and Julia only knew what was about to happen, they would know their decision to pray big things was going to change their lives forever!" I get a lot of joy out of thinking about the heavenly audience that cheers on Christians in their endeavors and cheers on non-Christians toward faith in Jesus Christ.

Ryan and I knew we wanted more out of life, but we needed to know how to actually get more. I'm not going to overspiritualize or hide our intention—we definitely wanted more out of life. We wanted more opportunities, more blessings, more purpose, more influence, more of a story. We just wanted *more*. And because of our faith in Jesus Christ, we were able to call the God of all the universe "Abba, Father" and ask Him for our heart's desires (Rom. 8:15).

Dream Big

That night, Ryan and I decided to write a list of twenty things we wanted. We have no shame in openly saying that was our goal: to get things we wanted. Yes, they ultimately turned into prayer requests, but first they were dreams and desires we had for our lives.

If this process seems unspiritual to you, then I would ask you to consider 1 John 5:14–15, which says, "This is the confidence which we have before Him, that, if we ask anything according to His will, He hears us. And if we know that He hears us in whatever we ask, we know that we have the requests which we have asked from Him." We will get into the theological ins and outs of this concept later, but here is the bottom line: the Bible dares us to pray for anything and everything, and it says God will give us what we ask when our requests are according to His will. The ball is in our court.

> *The Bible dares us to pray for anything and everything, and it says God will give us what we ask when our requests are according to His will.*

The Plan

How did Ryan and I come up with our list, you may ask? We started with the question my dad encourages his congregation to use in order to discover their purpose: If money were no issue and you knew you could not fail, what would you want to have happen in your career, relationships, and life? We then came up with twenty dreams for our lives.

We turned these twenty dreams into twenty prayer requests and then committed to praying for each request on the list both together and separately multiple times a day until God answered. These were not vague prayers. They were as specific as, "Please give us multiples" and "Please give us three biological children." These were two separate prayer requests that I never imagined God would put together to result in triplets.

Two principles guided our twenty-item prayer list plan: we were going to pray specifically, and we were going to pray persistently. The idea to pray specifically was spurred on by my favorite prayer quote. In his forty-day prayer challenge, entitled *Draw the Circle*, author Mark Batterson says, "The greatest tragedy in life is the prayers that go unanswered simply because they go unasked."[3]

The idea to pray persistently came from my favorite character in the Bible—the persistent widow. I love the persistent widow because she makes being super annoying a spiritual personality trait deemed appropriate and worthy of a chapter in the Bible. If you are unfamiliar with the story or need a refresher, allow me the honor of sharing her remarkable story with you.

In Luke 18, Jesus told the parable of the persistent widow to the disciples "to show that at all times they ought to pray and not to lose heart" (v. 1).

In a certain city there was a judge who did not fear God and did not respect man. There was a widow in that city, and she kept coming to him, saying, "Give me legal protection from my opponent." For a while he was unwilling; but afterward he said to himself, "Even though I do not fear God nor respect man, yet because this widow bothers me, I will give her legal protection, otherwise by continually coming she will wear me out." And the Lord said, "Hear what the unrighteous judge said; now, will not God bring about justice for His elect who cry to Him day and night, and will He delay long over them? I tell you that He will bring about justice for them quickly. However, when the Son of Man comes, will He find faith on the earth?" (vv. 2–8)

My favorite verse in this parable is verse 4: "Because this widow bothers me, I will give her legal protection." The persistent widow inspires me because she did not give up. She went after her heart's desire. This woman knew what she needed and went after it continually with all she had. She persistently bothered the one person who could grant her request until he answered her. How much more will the God who tells us to ask Him for our heart's desires listen and happily, readily, boldly answer the requests of His children?

I Dare You, and So Does God

I've often heard it said, "Aim for nothing, and you will hit it every time." This familiar saying haunts me every time I hear it. If I aim for nothing, then my experiences, relationships, and life will result in nothing. And that would be a shame, because God promises to give us everything we need, if only we will ask.

I want to be able to say at the end of my life that I did not give up. I want to be able to say that, to the best of my ability, I was persistent, relentless, and fearless in proclaiming the gospel of Jesus Christ. I want to be able to say that, regardless of what did or did not happen in my life, I kept praying, I kept believing, and I kept telling as many people as possible about Jesus until the moment I went home to meet my Savior face-to-face. I do not want anyone to turn to me on Judgment Day and say, "Why didn't you tell me about Jesus?" I want to pray and live in a way that allows God to pour out His blessings, opportunities, protection, and favor on me and my family.

I want to make the absolute most out of every opportunity I am given. I want to pray big things that result in seeing God do big things, more than anything I can hope or imagine. I want more out of this life, and I'm guessing you do too!

I do not want to miss out on anything in life because I simply did not take the time to ask God for what I need, dream, or want. James 4:2 says, "You do not have because you do not ask." It really does not get more straightforward, challenging, and daring than that!

Yes, God dares us to ask big things of Him. Instead of explaining Scriptures away, let's start claiming the promises of God for our lives, families, children, and dreams. This is a fun, practical, and hopefully inspiring book to get you excited to pray, to dream, and to want more for your life. My prayer is that through reading our story of God's faithfulness and creativity, you are challenged and encouraged to ask God to do immeasurably more in your life.

> *God dares us to ask big things of Him.*

This is a dare book. I dare you to do the things the Bible actually says and see what will happen in your life. I dare you to ask God fervently to make your late-night prayers and heartfelt dreams a reality.

I dare you to pray big things!

2

Is Anybody Up There?

We are not necessarily doubting that God will do the best for us; we are wondering how painful the best will turn out to be.

C. S. Lewis

We're going to lose this baby—I just know it," I lamented to Ryan. This was our third pregnancy in a matter of nine months, after miscarrying the previous two pregnancies. Ironically, I was soon to leave for an out-of-state speaking trip on which I was going to speak on depression, anxiety, and the topic "Why God allows suffering."

"Stop being so negative, Julia," Ryan responded sternly. "You don't know that is going to happen."

"I'm not being negative; I'm being practical," I protested. "I just know that I'm going to miscarry while I'm alone and out of the state this weekend. I need to be prepared, and this is God's way of preparing me. He is telling me it is coming, so I can decide ahead of time how I'm going to handle it."

As it turned out, I did lose baby number three the night before I left to go out of town.

What Do You Believe about God?

Three miscarriages were certainly not what Ryan and I had planned when we began our prayer journey that New Year's Eve. Every miscarriage coincided with a huge spiritual milestone in our family. Our worst season personally was our best season in ministry. We lost our first baby during an event where I had one hundred teenagers in my backyard and spoke to them about how God had called them to live a legacy in their exact place in life. We lost our second baby right before the greatest evangelism initiative our student ministry had ever seen, when teenagers were witnessing on Friday nights in malls and stopping to share Christ with Muslims on the street, and we saw one hundred and thirty people witnessed to by teenagers on fire for Christ. We lost our third baby while I was teaching at a women's conference on "Why God allows suffering." On top of this, I had thirteen pregnant friends announce their pregnancies, post super cute gender-reveal videos, and invite me to their baby showers.

To us, this felt like another dagger in what seemed like an unending attack or attempt to mock our faith. Once the struggle starts, it's too late to try to muster up spiritual thoughts and feelings. When the doctor's bad report comes, when the job is lost, when the spouse leaves, we are running on spiritual fumes.

Theologian and author A. W. Tozer once said, "What comes into our minds when we think about God is the most important thing about us."[1] We are all going to have times we question God. We will question His goodness. We will question His plan. We may even question His existence. The exciting thing about this truth is that we already know what we are to think about God. The questions are certain, but so are the answers. In the Bible, God has already told us who He is, what He thinks, how He acts, and how much He loves us.

So, why have so many of my counseling clients and teenagers in our student ministry become very angry upon hearing this Tozer quote? Why did you possibly stir in your seat as you read it? Perhaps it's because we don't want to believe that God has that much control over our lives. Maybe the unrest is because we don't want to surrender to the idea that our lives are bigger than we are. Determining who we believe God is and how He works will determine how we handle tragedy, how we handle blessing, how we handle doubts, and how we handle life.

> *Determining who we believe God is and how He works will determine how we handle tragedy, how we handle blessing, how we handle doubts, and how we handle life.*

Hebrews 6:18–19 tells us, "So that by two unchangeable things in which *it is impossible for God to lie*, we who have taken refuge would have strong encouragement to take hold of the hope set before us. This hope we have as an anchor of the soul, a hope both sure and steadfast." How wonderful that God cannot lie! This means we can trust Him even when we don't understand why things are going on in our lives. Deciding who we believe God to be is the most important thing about us.

This choice has to be made before the tragedy, before the pain, before the questions, before the heartache. We must decide what we think about God and choose what we believe about Him before our beliefs are challenged, questioned, or threatened. This is the order that will help preserve your faith: decide what you think about God, then live it out when difficult times come. This firm foundation is vital for spiritual survival and for dream survival.

Deciding to hold on to the dreams God has given us even when we lose pregnancies, jobs, friends, or status is what sets dreamers apart. Refusing to let go when everything in and around us is tempting us to do so is what will ensure we experience the life we have always dreamed of. Anyone can quit, but dreamers persist.

I had to choose to believe that God is good, He is in control, and He loves me in order to keep going during our season of miscarriages and loss. This is also the choice *you* have to make to keep going.

The Necessity of Our Emotions

One of my favorite clients, who will forever hold a special place in my heart, is the first parent I ever counseled who had lost her child to suicide. Let's call her Stacy. Stacy had what some people in the clinic were claiming was an unusual state of calmness and understanding surrounding the loss of her daughter. The staff decided she was probably overspiritualizing the tragedy, which was something we saw all too often, and we needed to get her to feel her pain instead of explaining it away. "She has to be mad at God," the therapists reasoned in our weekly staff meeting. "There is no way she is that much at peace already."

I remember sitting with her for many weeks as she explained how she still loved God and believed He was good, despite the unimaginable tragedy of losing her child to suicide. I tried to see if there was more to the story—more grief to process, more emotions left unturned—but week after week, nothing seemed to be surfacing.

One day I asked Stacy to write a letter to God. She was extremely reluctant to do so, which showed that I had stumbled upon the perfect assignment for her. For days, she claimed she'd forgotten to do the assignment, until one day she finally came in with her letter to God. Through tears in her eyes and lumps in her throat, she read the letter she wrote to her Savior. In the letter she admitted that she hated God for taking her daughter, but she knew God understood her pain because He had lost His child too.

Wow! What a perfect example of feeling pain while claiming scriptural truth. Yes, God understands our pain. He understands our questions. He even heard His own Son, Jesus, question Him as our Savior hung dying from the cross: "My God, My God, why have You forsaken Me?" (Matt. 27:46). God understands our hurt. He says to you and to me, *I love you, and I understand.*

> God understands our hurt. He says to you and to me, I love you, and I understand.

Let me insert here that the point of this story is not to get you to be mad at God. The point is to encourage you to be honest with God about any anger, hurt, sadness, or disappointment you may have toward Him. He already knows if you are angry with Him. We rarely admit any negative emotion we feel toward God because it can seem sacrilegious. I admit I constantly waver between wanting to focus on understanding the spiritual "why" behind an incident versus actually allowing myself to feel the hurt, pain, and sadness it causes. I think as Christians and as humans, we are allowed to do both, and in order to thrive in our Christian lives, we have to do both.

God never tells us to avoid our emotions. On the contrary, God created our emotions. Psalm 62:8 encourages us, "Trust in Him at all times, O people; pour out your heart before Him; God is a refuge for us." It's okay to cry out to God on the bathroom floor after another negative pregnancy test. It's okay to scream in your car out of frustration over another year of watching a child rebel against God. It's okay to tell God that you are overwhelmed and angry because you don't understand.

I used to teach a class on emotions several times a week at the Christian psychiatric hospital where I counseled. I would draw a diagram explaining that all emotions originate from a thought. This is the basis of cognitive behavioral therapy. The theory holds that in order to change your behavior and emotions, you must first change your thought pattern and worldview. The order of progression is Worldview → Thought → Emotion → Behavior. When we only recognize one of these influences on our behavior, we tend to ignore the rest. For example, it's easy to know when we feel angry, but it's sometimes difficult to know what our worldview and thoughts are that produce the emotion of anger.

We Cannot Separate Our Theology from Our Feelings

During my struggle with infertility, I noticed myself gradually reading my Bible less and less. I wasn't too hard on myself about it—until I realized I needed to practice what I preached and figure out the thoughts and feelings that were leading to my action of not reading the Bible. As I reflected on my situation and my heart, I realized I was angry at God because I thought He had been unjust. Theologically, I knew God was not unjust. Romans 9:14 tells us, "There is no injustice with God." But because I was unable to carry a pregnancy to term, I felt slighted by Him, and that feeling kept me from wanting to spend time with Him.

We cannot separate our theology from our feelings. I'm not saying that our feelings should dictate what we believe about God but rather, as humans, our feelings and thoughts about God go hand in hand.

Take, for example, the woman sitting in church who hears the pastor preach time and again that God loves her and cares for her. She intellectually believes this, nods her head as the pastor speaks, and may even whisper an "Amen" here and there. But in the back of her mind, she quietly wonders, *If God really loves me, then why did He let me suffer abuse as a child?* She doesn't really spend much time with God outside of church services because her feelings and theology do not match. In order to totally heal from her past hurts, this woman has to adopt the "You have to feel it to heal it" mantra.

It was easier for me to keep God at a distance than to accept He was 100 percent responsible for the loss of our babies. I didn't begin to experience emotional and spiritual healing until I finally told God, "I know You are good. I know

You love me. But I'm mad at You for letting this happen. Please help me not to stay this way and to see things how You want me to see them."

At the end of the day, we all want a God who is responsible, who knows what He is doing, and who has a plan in the pain. There is comfort in knowing we aren't the victim of random circumstances but instead are important players in God's ultimate story of redemption.

We aren't the victim of random circumstances but instead are important players in God's ultimate story of redemption.

If you have wondered if God is up there, you aren't alone. According to one Barna Group study, two-thirds of professing Christians have doubted their faith at some point.[2] The study found that stopping spiritual practices such as attending church, praying, and reading the Bible was commonplace for those experiencing doubt. Yet when we experience the difficult circumstances that come into our lives and cause doubt, that's when we need God the most. The truth is, it is always hard to do the things that help us the most: forgiving others, reading the Bible, eating vegetables. The temptation to openly run away from God or discreetly retreat from Him is real. We have to fight that urge. Our faith and our families depend on it.

As Henry Ford reportedly said, "Whether you think you can, or you think you can't—you're right." To those who think this philosophy sounds overly simplistic, consider the following verse. The Bible tells us of the connection between thoughts and identity in Proverbs 23:7, which says, "For as [a person] thinks within himself, so he is." What does this verse mean for Christians who believe that God has ordained every detail of our lives from the beginning of time? The connection of our actions and God's sovereign plan is a mystery this side of heaven. God cares about what we think, and our thoughts influence the outcomes of our lives.

Joseph—An Example of Refusing to Let Go of God-Given Dreams

When I think of a person in the Bible who exemplifies refusing to let go of his dreams, even in the face of difficult circumstances, I think of the Old Testament character Joseph. Joseph was the great-grandson of Abraham and one of the twelve sons of Jacob.

In Genesis 37, God gave Joseph a dream that someday he would be a leader over his older brothers. As you can imagine, they did not respond well to the news that their little brother would eventually reign over them. The Bible says, "They hated him even more for his dreams and for his words" (v. 8). Then God gave Joseph another dream, this time making it clear that he would reign over not only his brothers but also his parents. In response to this dream, "his brothers were jealous of him, but his father kept the saying in mind" (v. 11).

Joseph's brothers mockingly called him a "dreamer" (v. 19) and conspired to kill him. While those closest to him hated him, mocked him, and planned to hurt him, Joseph clung to his dreams. And those God-given dreams sustained him through the next season of trials, abandonment, slavery, and rejection.

When we read Joseph's story, it's important for us to remember that Joseph heard from God before he heard his brothers plot to take his life. Joseph received his dreams before his slavery. And Joseph refused to let go of them when all evidence pointed to his dreams being over, done, and possibly the result of just having a lot of chocolate before bed.

Your God-given dreams will sustain you too, no matter what your future holds.

God often gives us the dream first to help prepare us with hope for the future. The dreams are what sustained Joseph during extremely difficult circumstances. And your God-given dreams will sustain you too, no matter what your future holds.

Living between the Smile and the Frown

One of the worst tasks of adulthood is having to go to the Department of Motor Vehicles and renew your driver's license. The process takes forever. And then there is the minor detail of the picture for the license that you have to use and see and show to others nearly every day of your life.

I recently had to go in person to renew my license and was prepared to take a great picture—or at least, hopefully, one that I wouldn't dread showing the cashier at Target. As the lady taking the picture started to count to three, I flashed my biggest and best smile. She stopped at the number two and said, "Hey, were you a cheerleader or something? Your smile is really fake!" In the split second it took for me to process what she was saying, my smile dropped to a frown and, yes, just in that moment she snapped the picture!

I think most of us live our lives between the flashy cheer-leading smile that comes when we can see God moving and the frown that seems to be our pervasive disposition over the days, weeks, months, and even years as we search for God's presence in the midst of our questions, suffering, and pain. Let's be honest: it's easy to smile and sing praises to God when things are going our way. It's easy to proclaim, "God is good!" when we can see His tangible blessings and His work in our lives. But what are we supposed to do when things don't go according to plan? When God doesn't seem to be answering, when the diagnosis isn't good, when our spouse isn't repentant, when we are stuck in the same struggle—what are we to do?

Some Christians seem to adopt the Nat King Cole "Smile" philosophy and put on a smile no matter what, even though their hearts are breaking. If we follow that philosophy, we will smile our way right out of church, right out of our faith, and right out of our dreams.

How our prayers affect God's plan is a mystery, but it doesn't change the truth that our prayers do matter and affect the outcome of events in our lives. Even during the most difficult year of my life so far, I didn't doubt God's goodness. I refused to do so. Instead, I chose to stop treating the Bible as a book of suggestions and started claiming and believing it as the only way my life would ever work. It was the only choice I had, and it's the only choice you have.

> *Our prayers do matter and affect the outcome of events in our lives.*

What would happen if we really believed the Bible—if we really claimed the promises and believed the verses we recite

to others and post on social media? How much encouragement and strength and perspective would infiltrate our lives
if we truly believed the childhood song "Jesus loves me this
I know, for the Bible tells me so"?

Difficult times aren't a matter of "if" but of "when." In
1 Peter 4:12–14, the apostle Peter explains the certainty of
difficult times:

> Beloved, do not be surprised at the fiery ordeal among you,
> which comes upon you for your testing, as though some
> strange thing were happening to you; but to the degree
> that you share the sufferings of Christ, keep on rejoicing,
> so that also at the revelation of His glory you may rejoice
> with exultation. If you are reviled for the name of Christ,
> you are blessed, because the Spirit of glory and of God
> rests on you.

The good news is that while hard times are certain, our
spiritual growth can be just as certain. The most common
outcome for Christians who are honest about their spiritual
doubts is a closer relationship with Christ. Roxanne Stone,
editor in chief of the Barna Group, explained it well:

> Spiritual doubt has been a reality of the Christian journey
> since the disciples—and today is no different. . . . Just like
> first century Christians, their twenty-first century counter-
> parts question aspects of their theology, doubt the existence
> of God and mourn his seeming absence during hard times.
> Doubt remains a flip side on the same coin as faith. For the
> majority of Christians, this inevitable doubt is a catalyst to
> spiritual growth. This should lead pastors and spiritual men-
> tors to view seasons of spiritual doubt in their constituents
> as fertile soil—not as dangerous ground.[3]

Doubt is certain, but so are answers, both in this life and in the next. If we knew everything about why anything happened, we would have no interest in God. We would have no need to trust Him, no reason to spend time with Him, no reason to long for eternity. The mystery is part of the plan and part of the surprise.

Take Action

How do we stay devoted to our dreams, our family, and our faith when we are in the midst of our holding cell, like the one Joseph experienced?

Be Honest about Your Feelings and Questions

First, when we are experiencing doubts about God, we must be honest about our feelings and questions. While Joseph's questioning of God is not recorded in the biblical account of his life, I'm willing to bet Joseph had more than one heart-to-heart conversation with God during his time in captivity, because while Joseph was a great biblical example of faith and perseverance, he was also human. I'm also willing to bet this because of where Joseph ended up. Being honest lets us move on in our relationship with God. Hiding our doubts and questions will keep us stuck and powerless. We will not reach our dreams by accident. We will not end up with a stronger faith after times of trial by default. This is an active stance—a battle.

Decide Who God Is and What You Believe about Him

Second, now is the time to decide who God is. I remember going to get a very important medical test done, a defining test that would basically tell my husband and me which one of us was to blame for our infertility issues. I remember God so clearly telling me I needed to write out a declaration of my beliefs before we got the results. I sat at the kitchen counter with my computer, and for about twenty minutes before the doctor's appointment, I wrote out everything I believed to be true about myself, about my marriage, about Ryan, and most importantly about God. I did this so that no

Today is the day to decide to be all-in for God.

matter what the results were—whether I couldn't have children, Ryan couldn't have children, or there was some horrible illness to blame—I would be able to look back and read what I knew to be true before the other shoe dropped.

Joshua 24:15 charges us, "Choose for yourselves today whom you will serve." Today is the day to decide to be all-in for God.

Take Captive Thoughts That Suggest Otherwise

Third, in our seasons of doubt, we need to identify and deal with thoughts that are contrary to what we know to be true about God and His plan for our life. While he was in prison for a crime he didn't commit, after being sold by his brothers into slavery, Joseph continued to believe God was in control. When the cupbearer talked about his dream to Joseph, Joseph replied, "Do not interpretations belong to God?" (Gen. 40:8). Abandoned by his family, alone in a foreign country, and wrongfully sentenced to prison, Joseph certainly had an excuse to wonder if God was up there. Surely no one would have blamed Joseph if he had taken a hiatus from telling others about God. Yet, even in the midst of this difficult and unfair situation, Joseph remained faithful to God and confident in God's power.

I'm sure Joseph had moments alone in his cell, feeling the exhaustion and isolation of prison, remembering his brothers' betrayal, remembering his prophetic dream of ruling over his brothers, when he was tempted to doubt the goodness of God. But declaring God's Word and His goodness to others can be great reinforcement of our faith in times of hardship. I'm not talking about empty platitudes. I'm talking about using the opportunity of our struggle to point others to Christ.

We are not responsible for how God looks. He has every right to remedy situations or to let our worst fears come to be. And even if He doesn't answer how we want, God is still good and on His throne. We are responsible for our faith and actions. We know Satan attacks our thoughts. This was his primary tactic with Jesus in the wilderness—to get Jesus to question God's goodness and God's Word. Questioning these two pillars of the faith will be our primary temptations in times of trials as well.

The Bible commands us to "put on the Lord Jesus Christ, and make no provision for the flesh" (Rom. 13:14) and to take "every thought captive to the obedience of Christ" (2 Cor. 10:5). God never asks us to do things that aren't possible. He tells us to take control of our thoughts because we are, in fact, able to do so. Expressing our feelings is an important part of healing, but we cannot get stuck in our emotions. Feeling cannot replace thinking. We have no choice in our feelings, but we have great choice in our thoughts.

> *We have no choice in our feelings, but we have great choice in our thoughts.*

49

During my years in postgraduate work at the esteemed Meier Clinics, I would often hear psychologists affirm this phenomenon in research on brain function and intrusive thoughts, concluding that humans actually have 95 percent control over their thoughts. Let's say the remaining 5 percent are spiritual warfare or automatic responses from trauma and triggers. The theology and psychology are clear: we have a choice in the majority of what we believe about our situation, about others, and about God.

Refuse to Give Up on Your Dreams and Prayers

Fourth, if we know our dreams come from God, and if our dreams have been confirmed by others who know us and love Jesus, then we must hold fast to them and refuse to give up until God fulfills what He has promised us. I'm willing to bet Joseph spent a considerable amount of time recalling his dreams. Dreams keep us going.

At every turn, we see Joseph looking for opportunities to be rescued and for his situation to be redeemed. He stayed faithful but also stayed active. We will look more at this in future chapters. The bottom line is that Joseph refused to give up.

There was a time in my graduate school years when every single morning seemed like a battle to go to class. I'm convinced even kindergarteners can relate to the struggle. It got so bad that every morning I would read this quote for motivation to keep going:

Nothing in this world can take the place of persistence. Talent will not: nothing is more common than unsuccessful men with talent. Genius will not: unrewarded genius is almost a proverb. Education will not: the world is full of educated derelicts. Persistence and determination alone are omnipotent.[4]

Persistence will set us apart and above the struggles that threaten our dreams.

Why Does God Allow Suffering?

"How can a good God allow suffering?" is a question that spans generations and centuries. While this question can seem unspiritual at times, even Jesus, the Son of God, cried out, "My God, My God, why have You forsaken Me?" (Matt. 27:46) as He hung dying on the cross. This makes questioning God's presence seem almost fated for those closest to Him. After all, as children of God, we have tasted His goodness. We know His power. We have a relationship with Him—and so perhaps we are more likely to feel His perceived absence than those who do not?

I have seen Romans 8:28—"God causes all things to work together for good to those who love God, to those who are called according to His purpose"—quoted at times that make people scream in outrage. It is a hard truth to accept and a verse that needs to be carefully and appropriately quoted. However, during times of tragedy, questions, and suffering, biblical truth is the only true comfort we have in this life.

There was nothing good about Jesus's dying on the cross. The disciples were terrified, the cause of Christ was halted, and Jesus was dead. But that was the perspective of Good Friday. On Sunday morning, when Jesus rose from the dead, people finally understood that all things really had happened for a reason—Jesus had been murdered so that we could have eternal life.

God did not answer Jesus's prayer before the cross to "remove this cup from Me" (Luke 22:42), but Jesus "learned obedience from the things which He suffered" (Heb. 5:8). As pastor F. B. Meyer states in his book *Abraham or the Obedience of Faith*, "Trials are, therefore, God's vote of confidence in us."[5] Though our struggles often surprise us, they never surprise God. God is in heaven cheering us on and equipping us for every battle on the horizon. He knows we are more than capable to conquer the seemingly impossible quest set before us.

> *God gives us the strength to pray big things even in the furnace so we can see our prayers, our families, and our souls brightened by the fire.*

Running to God instead of away from God in the midst of suffering is not a natural response. It is the supernatural response that God equips His children with as we stare grief, uncertainty, fear, and sometimes Satan himself in the face. Warren Wiersbe reminds believers,

> When God puts His own people into the furnace, He keeps His eye on the clock and His hand on the thermostat. He knows how long and how much. We may question why He does it to begin with or why He doesn't turn down the heat or even turn it off; but our questions are only evidences of unbelief. Job 23:10 is the answer: "But He knows the way that I take; when He has tested me, I shall come forth as gold" (NKJV). *Gold does not fear the fire.* The furnace can only make the gold purer and brighter.[6]

God never abandons us in our time of need. In times of struggle and heartache, He holds us more closely, speaks to us more loudly, and comforts us more deeply. God gives us the strength to pray big things even in the furnace so we can see our prayers, our families, and our souls brightened by the fire.

3

Work Hard, Pray Harder

Pray as if everything depended on God and work as if everything depended on you.

St. Ignatius of Loyola

John Quincy Adams believed God called him to end slavery in America. After serving a four-year term as president, he decided to run for a seat in the House of Representatives, where he became famous for giving sledgehammer-style messages at our nation's capitol. Adams would deliver compelling arguments and convicting biblical truths about the evils of slavery. He was so convinced that this was God's plan for his life that he talked to everyone he could about the necessity of changing this injustice in our country. Adams lived with vigor and courage as a man called by God for the specific purpose of righting one of the worst injustices of our nation's history.

All of this came to a screeching halt on February 21, 1848, when Adams collapsed on the floor of the House of Representatives, having suffered a stroke. He fell into a coma and died two days later without ever seeing the end of slavery. His last words supposedly were, "This is the end of earth, but I am content."[1]

Did Adams mishear God's calling on his life? Did he imagine that he had a grand purpose that in fact was nothing but a grand illusion? Neither. What John Quincy Adams didn't know at the time was, while God did not plan for him to see the end of slavery in America, He had placed in the back of the room, listening to Adams, a young congressman who would eventually become the president who did free the slaves.

Abraham Lincoln said the sermons on slavery by John Quincy Adams were the most memorable speeches he heard during his years as a congressman. In an article exploring Adams's influence on Lincoln, historian Robert Samuelson observed, "We may say, to simplify, that [Adams] made Lincoln possible."[2] John Quincy Adams influenced the president who ended slavery by working as if this important milestone depended solely on him while relying on God to ultimately bring about the end of slavery in America.

You will always win when you care about what God cares about.

You will always win when you care about what God cares about.

A Purpose beyond Our Pain

Our worst year personally was one of our best years in ministry. The year we miscarried three babies was also the year that the church where we serve, First Baptist Church of Dallas, launched our "Tell the World" initiative for our student ministry. Young men and women, ages twelve to eighteen, were equipped and encouraged to share the gospel with anyone and everyone, and the result was nothing short of remarkable. The students caught the vision of Romans 1:16, which says, "I am not ashamed of the gospel, for it is the power of God for salvation to everyone who believes, to the Jew first and also to the Greek." We had thirteen-year-olds organizing Friday night witnessing groups at malls and in downtown Dallas. Our students saw many of their friends, family members, and complete strangers accept Christ as their Savior. This was a fire that could not be put out. By the end of the three-month initiative, more than 150 people in our city had heard about Jesus Christ from someone who was not old enough to vote. Our students experienced firsthand the truth of Isaiah 55:11: "My word . . . goes forth from My mouth; it will not return to Me empty, without accomplishing what I desire, and without succeeding in the matter for which I sent it."

There is work to be done and people to be reached, and nothing can take that purpose away from you!

Ryan and I were faced with the undeniable truth that God had a ministry plan and purpose for us that was not contingent on our ability to stay pregnant. So we set our minds, hearts, and lives on caring about and working toward the only thing God has left us here to do—to tell people about Christ. There is work to be done and people to be reached, and nothing can take that purpose away from you!

Seeing Past Our Situation

When tragedy or even mere disappointment enters our lives, it is hard to see past our situation and past ourselves. Have you ever noticed how self-centered depressed people are? It seems like all they can do is talk about themselves. In his classic book on recovery, *Healing the Shame That Binds You*, Dr. John Bradshaw explains that depressed people always talk about themselves for the same reason people with a toothache always talk about their teeth: the pain is all they can think about, so it's all they can talk about.[3] Satan really plays into our pain. Though often our pain is supposed to be an opportunity for the Holy Spirit to shape our hearts to become more like Jesus Christ, it is also a time of great temptation to believe the lies that God is not good or active. In times of difficulty, it's easy to believe that God has put us on the shelf, benched us for another season.

Sometimes the best conversations happen "on the bench." The bench allows us to slow down, to watch what's happening, and to decide our strategy against our opponent. The bench also allows us to talk to the people we often miss during the game. I honestly sometimes miss the waiting time—the time where I could do nothing except have faith that God knew what He was doing when I didn't have a clue. But in reality, isn't that everything? I'm so thankful to have been taught by my father and lifelong pastor, "Waiting time doesn't have to be wasted time." When we experience loss, setbacks, bench time, loneliness, or uncertainty, it can be hard to see God and to feel that we are a part of His great story. The Bible says, "Hope deferred makes the heart sick" (Prov. 13:12), and hoping when our life seems to be halted is one of the most difficult tasks of the human spirit and of the Christian faith. Satan doesn't have to make us fall into some horrible habitual sin to miss our purpose in life. He only has to make us think we've been forgotten.

Sometimes God benches us, sometimes we bench ourselves, and sometimes Satan wants to make us think we've been benched, forgotten by the One who promises to "not fail you or forsake you" (Josh. 1:5). This was the tactic used by Satan to tempt Jesus in the wilderness. Soldiers who don't fight don't win wars. People who don't believe in the war don't become skilled in using their weapons and are defeated before the fight begins.

During our year of miscarriages, I was constantly reminded of the reality of spiritual warfare. Without giving Satan too much thought or mention, the truth is that we really do have an enemy who "prowls around like a roaring lion, seeking someone to devour" (1 Pet. 5:8). At some point, it will feel like he has set his teeth in you. I remember someone who missed the point of the character Aslan in the Chronicles of Narnia, saying, "Don't let your kids watch that movie; the lion, Aslan, is scary!" In this critically acclaimed book series by C. S. Lewis, the character of Aslan represents Christ in His gentleness and His fierceness. Lewis writes,

> Wrong will be right, when Aslan comes in sight,
> At the sound of his roar, sorrows will be no more,
> When he bares his teeth, winter meets its death,
> And when he shakes his mane, we shall have spring again.[4]

Aslan does not represent the peaceful, minds His own business, tolerant of every lifestyle, and accepting of every religion Jesus that is the figment of the imagination of those who have forgotten or who have never known the Jesus of the Bible. While Satan is strong, Jesus is stronger. Satan knows how to tempt us, but Jesus knows how to vindicate us. Our job is to keep going.

Satan knows how to tempt us, but Jesus knows how to vindicate us. Our job is to keep going.

I always thought the saying "Do the next right thing" was a tad simplistic, but sometimes it's all we can do. Keep working. Keep trusting. Keep believing. Keep praying. Keep going. Anyone can quit. To keep on keeping on can be our greatest legacy and testimony to the lost world.

If Satan can make us believe we've been forgotten by God, he is close to winning the story of our life. The bitterness of believing that the God who gave His Son for us is not good is too much for our souls to bear. It's such a contradiction that we cannot survive spiritually while believing this. We must choose to fight. We must choose to keep going. Satan will keep using the same tricks on us as long as they work. As I have often heard said, "Make Satan try something new."

When I realized I was going to miscarry on the weekend I would be teaching the topic "Why God allows suffering" to hundreds of women, my pain was so real and I was so sad, but the irony and the obvious way Satan was trying to attack were honestly laughable. I resolved that year to believe the Bible. The struggles girded me with even more certainty and fight to proclaim the goodness of God. I realized that testing is an honor. We must switch out of a victim mentality and into a victor mentality.

Something Big Is about to Happen

During the year of our miscarriages, I had lunch with my sister, Dorothy, and we discussed all that was happening: the miscarriages and the seeming halt to some significant dreams of our immediate family members. Then she said something I'll never forget. She looked at me and said, "Julia, I think something really big is about to happen." This was a year before the triplets were born, before my dad became a presidential adviser, and before Ryan and I were cast in a reality TV show that gave us the ability to talk about Jesus Christ on a national platform. How did Dorothy know?

Dorothy is not some kind of modern-day prophetess, but she understands the spiritual progression of events. Temptation, struggles, trials, and persecution usually come before the blessing. If we figure out that sequence, we will not be swayed in our beliefs. While the trials will be hard, our victory is certain.

What would happen in your family and in your faith if you kept going? If you refused to give up no matter what you were faced with? The Bible encourages us in James 1:12 that our trials are not in vain: "Blessed is the one who perseveres under trial because, having stood the test, that person will receive the crown of life that the Lord has promised to those who love him" (NIV).

I remember almost feeling proud in the midst of the year of so many miscarriages that Satan found Ryan and me worthy targets of discouragement. I also started to wonder, with excitement in the midst of pain, about what lay ahead that Satan had set his sights on destroying us. At times, it seemed as though God and Satan were waging war and fighting for control over my family and my faith.

With every miscarriage, God provided some unique form of encouragement. I remember one time in particular, after I lost a pregnancy, I went to my email to see that I had been booked in Maine to speak to one thousand teenagers about why their lives matter. This kind of encouragement from God is not exclusively for me but it is available to every person with a broken heart but a hope-filled spirit who refuses to take his or her eyes off of Jesus Christ.

A Record of God's Faithfulness

I just finished writing in what has to be my favorite journal to date. On the last page I wrote Joshua 4:6–7, which says,

> When your children ask in time to come, "What do those stones mean to you?" then you shall tell them that the waters of the Jordan were cut off before the ark of the covenant of the LORD. When it passed over the Jordan, the waters of the Jordan were cut off. So these stones shall be to the people of Israel a memorial forever. (ESV)

I accidentally read Joshua 4 twice in a row because I hadn't kept track of where I was in the book of Joshua, but I'm so glad I did! God reminded me that my purpose is to pass on the stories of His goodness and faithfulness to my children. If I had given up, there would have been no story; there would have been no children to whom to tell the story.

I decided to look back at my first entry in the journal, which I had written almost exactly a year before the triplets were born. It read, "Please make 2017 the best year ever!" I smile when I think of how God knows perfectly how to speak to our hearts and minds. He created us, after all, so He knows what will get our attention, what will stir our spirit, and what will change us for- ever. He also knows how much we can take and when we really need a win (or three!).

We are often just a journal's length away from our whole world completely changing.

My point is not to make you go through my journal chronologically but to show you that we are often just a journal's length away from our whole world completely changing.

Joseph—An Example of Hard Work

In prison, it would have been so easy for Joseph to have said to God, "You know, God, right now I just need a little me time. I'm sure you understand all you have put me through, and I've been so faithful for so long. Let's pick back up when you get me out of here, okay?" Of course, this is not what happened. Joseph held on to the dreams God had given him for guidance, for encouragement, and for direction, and he looked time and time again for ways God's promises would manifest in his life.

Joseph also worked hard. He didn't simply say, "Well, God, you said I would rule over my brothers, and now I'm in prison, so I'm just going to let you work this one out." Joseph was an active player in the story of his life. God doesn't need us, but He knows we will finish trials with so much more enthusiasm for Him when we actually have to live out our faith.

There is a happy partnership between faith and works. James declares in James 2:26, "Just as the body without the spirit is dead, so also faith without works is dead." We can say we have faith, but until we decide to go into our lives with a flashlight barely showing us the way versus a spotlight that shows us everything, we are all talk.

Perhaps one of the most profound verses in the faith journey of Abraham is Hebrews 11:8, which says, "By faith Abraham, when he was called, obeyed by going out to a place which he was to receive for an inheritance; and he went out, not knowing where he was going." Abraham obeyed, and he went. He had the right theology and the right game plan. As Christine Caine has said, "[God] does not ask, *Are you capable?* He asks, *Are you willing?*"[5]

Working toward our goals, taking up kingdom causes, continuing to dream, and choosing to act are extremely hard during the waiting season. But the decision to keep going, to keep fighting, to keep dreaming, and to keep praying big is what will ensure that our waiting time is not wasted time. Honesty, persistence, and focus are the name of the game for trying times.

So many times, as a therapist, I would have people tell me they just wanted to get over situations that had hurt them. They would mock the process of therapy and say, "I don't want to talk the issue to death; I just want to feel better." To which I would reply, "You have to feel it to heal it. You have to go through the pain to get over the pain." Choose to go with God through the journey. While the circumstance we are going through may be something we would never have written in our life plan, we have the ability to make it a journey we will never forget and wouldn't trade for the world.

We must be honest about our feelings so that we can move forward. We have to remain persistent in our life calling. We must stay focused on the goodness of God. Even though we may not understand why God has allowed something painful to occur, we will not let it be in vain.

I remember one time crying out to God after a heart-break and saying, "Lord, teach me what You want me to learn, so I never have to go through this again!" If God is who He says He is, then where we find ourselves never catches Him off guard. Nothing surprises God. There is so much comfort when we understand this truth. Wherever you find yourself today, regardless of how difficult your circumstances may be, in the grand scheme of things this place has been planned by God. That means you have something to do *today*—not something to do when you get married, get pregnant, find a new job, retire, and so forth. You have a God-given purpose this very day that is not contingent on your current circumstances. So, let's figure out what that purpose is!

Take Action

How do we keep moving forward when life seems to be pushing us three (or twenty!) steps backward?

Develop Your Life Purpose

God has certain biblical purposes that apply to all of us. For example, we don't have to wonder whether God wants us to become Christians. We don't have to pray about if we should stay sexually pure. These are things the Bible clearly states that God desires for all of us. Scripture says, "The Lord is not slow about His promise, as some count slowness, but is patient toward you, not wishing for any to perish but for all to come to repentance" (2 Pet. 3:9). People will perish because they have not accepted Christ as their Savior, but that is not God's ultimate desire for anyone.

We also know that God's will for all Christians is to share the gospel. In Matthew 28:19–20, Jesus commands us, "Go therefore and make disciples of all the nations, baptizing them in the name of the Father and the Son and the Holy Spirit, teaching them to observe all that I commanded you; and lo, I am with you always, even to the end of the age." This command is not for just some Christians who are super-evangelistic and naturally geared toward talking to strangers. The call to tell the world about Christ is for every follower of Jesus Christ. We are all called to tell as many people as possible how to get to heaven.

While God has many callings and commands that apply to everyone, He also has unique and personalized purposes for each of us that are adventures waiting to be discovered. My dad has an equation for helping people discover their purpose. He says that "passion + opportunity + need = purpose." This is why we don't have to worry that God might call us to something we have no interest in doing. God has given you your dreams, talents, and desires, which means He not only has a great plan for your life but also has equipped you with the personality, talent, and interests you need in order to accomplish this plan. His purpose will allow you to live without regrets and make the most out of everything with which He has gifted you.

I have heard Christians scoff at the phrase "Find out who you are." "All that matters is who God is, not who we are," I have heard people argue. But the truth is that God has made us all unique with individual gifts, opportunities, and purposes. We have to know how God made us in order to fully honor Him with our lives.

For example, I hate being alone. Period. It's a good thing I know this, because then I know any job that means I'll be spending a lot of time alone is not one for me. A job that goes completely against my personality makeup is not likely one that will honor God, because I'll be so miserable. Of course, we all have to go through tests and trials, but it's important for us to fully realize the person God has made us to be and own our gifts, traits, and abilities in the good times and the bad, wherever we go.

What are the things you are passionate about? What problems or causes stir your heart when you read about them?

We have a woman in our church, Suzie, who was so concerned about homeless people in Dallas in the winter that she dedicated herself to raising funds to give blankets to those living on the streets. She now organizes a citywide annual fund-raiser to help collect blankets for the winter. Suzie had a passion for the homeless and an opportunity to help make their lives better. Her passion and opportunity met a genuine, felt need of thousands of people. If you have no interest in science, God has probably not called you to find a cure for cancer. If you can't seem to ignore the tugging at your heart toward the needs of a certain group of people and find yourself constantly concerned or interested in them, then that concern probably does have something to do with your life purpose.

Ask God What He Has for You Today

What you want for your life right now may not be bad, evil, or sinful. Maybe what you want is even in the plan for what

God has for you. But it's not what God has given you yet. And this thing is keeping you stuck, miserable, and ineffective.

I remember being introduced to a whole subgroup of married adults who were struggling with infertility. I had no clue how many couples struggle with infertility for years, sometimes resulting in the end of their relationship. I also was interested in the different responses of couples who were struggling. Some couples seemed to have purpose outside of trying to get pregnant. They still served in church. They still had fun as a couple. They still were actively working toward kingdom purposes. But other couples could talk about little else besides trying to get pregnant. The topic consumed their conversations. The struggle took over their entire lives.

This trap is not just for people desiring children. Many singles talk about little else besides wanting to be in a relationship, and many businesspeople talk about little besides their next deal. While there is nothing wrong with these dreams, they keep many people stuck in their struggles instead of figuring out what God has for them today. I once heard a great quote about balancing our desires with God's plan: "God knows what we need, so if we don't have something, it's ultimately because we don't need it yet." God hasn't accidentally put us in our current situation. He has a purpose, and He has a plan. It's time to find out what that is.

God hasn't accidentally put us in our current situation. He has a purpose, and He has a plan.

Stay Committed and Obedient

When I was a child, I remember hearing in Sunday school that it was wrong to follow God just for the purpose of getting rewards in heaven. But let's be clear about something: you and I like rewards because God created us to like rewards. God told us about the rewards we will have in heaven to motivate us to work for them on earth. There is nothing in my heart that inherently makes me want to be nice to people who cut me off on the highway. And that's okay. It's okay to fight to stay obedient to Christ, because God has promised to reward us if we do so.

The Bible promises us there are rewards in this life and in the next life for enduring hardship, staying faithful in the midst of suffering, and following Christ. James 1:12 tells us, "Blessed is a man who perseveres under trial; for once he has been approved, he will receive the crown of life which the Lord has promised to those who love Him."

Elisabeth Elliot, missionary and widow of martyred missionary Jim Elliot, had a profound insight into obedience. She said,

> I would not be truthful if I did not admit that the price of knowing him, of putting faith in him, and of understanding who he is has sometimes seemed high to me. . . . But neither would I be a faithful witness if I did not also say that it's worth the price—it's infinitely worth the price—and that God will never fail you.[6]

There is a point to our obedience. There is a reward for our obedience. The times you most don't want to go to church, push yourself to go. When you're tempted to skip your daily Bible reading and prayer, try telling God how you honestly feel. Even when we can't see what God is doing, we can trust His heart. He is always working with our best in mind.

69

Map Out Your Life

I struggled with eating disorders for ten years before deciding to become a professional therapist. I went to many different programs, counselors, and doctors during my long struggle. I will never forget the program that best grabbed my attention and snapped me into the reality of the situation.

One of the first realities to disappear for people who struggle with eating disorders is the abstract idea of the future. All that seems to matter are the weight and food thoughts and struggles going on in that hour, sometimes in that minute. People with eating disorders are obsessed with the idea that one meal will change everything for the good or the bad. Therapists have to work to help patients see past their current state and look further down the road at their health, relationships, and life. Eating disorders are terrible best friends that don't love you back, lie to you, and cause you to forget that life is about more than weight and about more than today.

As a visual to help patients see their progress, there was a map that hung above the place where we had our meals. The patients were represented by little cutouts of princes and princesses. The map included different milestones that patients were trying to reach, represented by adventures commonly found in fairy tales. There was the labyrinth, the forest, and finally the castle. I could always look up at the map and know exactly where I was, where I needed to go, and what I needed to do in order to get there.

Since that time, I have started seeing my life as an adventure map with dragons to slay, rivers to swim, mountains to climb, and wars to be won. And best of all, there is a home better than a castle for those of us who know Christ.

I wonder what it would be like if we started realizing that our present state is only permanent if we let it be permanent. How many people lose sight of their dreams because they can't see that once we are through the forest of trials, there is a great field of wonder, awe, and clarity?

> *Our present state is only permanent if we let it be permanent.*

Let's do something fun that I doubt you have done before. Let's map out your life as if it were a children's storybook. Make a list of all the key events, struggles, and relationships that have shaped you, and then plot them out on your "life map." While I realize some of you will like this activity more than others, getting a mental picture of how God has journeyed with you and moved you along will be a huge encouragement to keep going. Then, honestly evaluate where you are, decide what needs to happen in order for you to move forward, and then dream about what could be waiting on the other side.

I present suicide prevention programs in junior high schools, high schools, and churches. Why do I choose to have what so many people call an incredibly sad job? It's simple: I want to help people fight the lie that they have nothing to live for. The primary factor in suicide is hopelessness. This means the primary way to overcome suicidal thoughts is to have hope.

While you may not be struggling with thoughts of suicide today, you may be having a hard time keeping going. That means, my friend, that it's time to dream. Mark on your life map what could be waiting for you on the other side of your current situation. Maybe you recently ended a relationship. Draw on the other side the husband or wife waiting for you.

Maybe, like Ryan and I were, you find yourself grieved by infertility or miscarriage. Draw the children God may have for you on the other side of this trial. I'm not saying this art project will determine your future. I'm simply trying to remind you that you have a destiny. And if you keep God at the center of your desires, plans, prayers, and dreams, your destiny will be better than anything you can imagine.

Ephesians 3:20–21 has been the cry of our hearts these past two years: "Now to Him who is able to do far more abundantly beyond all that we ask or think, according to the power that works within us, to Him be the glory in the church and in Christ Jesus to all generations forever and ever. Amen." In my wildest dreams, I never would have drawn triplets on the other side of three miscarriages, but God did. God can and will do more than you hope or imagine when you give yourself completely to Him.

When I have been at my lowest point spiritually, questioning God and wondering the purpose of my life, I have heard a quiet whisper in my heart and mind: *But what if I keep going?*

What is waiting for you if you keep doing, keep going, and keep praying big things?

What journey is out there for you? What is waiting for you if you keep doing, keep going, and keep praying big things? Refuse to give up despite the defeat, the setbacks, and the losses. Set your sights on finding nothing less than the adventure waiting for you.

4

Don't Just Pray

With great power comes great responsibility.
Uncle Ben, *Spider-Man*

Humanity has always been fascinated by the idea of an alternate reality. Whether we are talking about superheroes, other worlds, or special powers, we, mere mortals, are obsessed with wanting there to be more than this life. We want more meaning, more purpose, and more power. The megasuccess of the *Star Wars* franchise, as well as the off-the-charts box-office success of the Marvel superhero movies, reveal that people are fascinated with the idea of being able to figure out how to access more power.

The seemingly mythical idea that people are able to be more powerful, be more in touch, and make a bigger impact on the trajectory of history strikes a chord with us because it's true. People love alternate realities, yet many don't realize there actually is another world, with supernatural characters and powers waiting to be unleashed in our midst every moment of our lives. As we discussed in chapter 3, we are a part of a supernatural war, whether we know it or not. We have incredible power through Jesus Christ, but it's up to us to unleash it.

We have incredible power through Jesus Christ, but it's up to us to unleash it.

I often wonder how many different movies about the same superhero can be made. I'm convinced there eventually will be a *Batman 27*. With every generation comes a new desire to conquer the world, and this desire was once in all of us. Maybe you still have it, or maybe you have lost it along the way. Maybe you have been told no too many times. It's time to find your way back to the adventure you were created to live. For a culture that is so infatuated with epic tales of superheroes, world powers colliding, and usually a love story mixed in for good measure, it seems counterintuitive that so many people are completely unaware of their own hidden powers.

The point of our lives is not to watch other people live their dreams. Far too many people today are so busy watching other people's lives through the lens of social media that they completely miss out on living their own lives. I don't want to miss my destiny, and I'm guessing you don't want to either!

Live with Power

In the 2002 movie *Spider-Man*, Uncle Ben wisely explains to his superhero nephew, "With great power comes great responsibility."[1] If you have put your faith and trust in Jesus

Christ for your salvation, then this quote is even more true for you than it is for Spider-Man. As Christians, we have great power and great responsibility. We have in us the same great power that resurrected Jesus from the dead. Having that kind of power means our lives should look different from those who do not have that power.

The "power" is the power of the Holy Spirit; the "responsibility" is the responsibility of those who have tasted the goodness of the Lord to make sure our lives are lived differently. We have the responsibility to further the gospel of Jesus Christ. Jesus said, "Let your light shine before men in such a way that they may see your good works, and glorify your Father who is in heaven" (Matt. 5:16).

We need to pray with power. We need to persist with power. We need to live with power. We need to look into our future and, as Proverbs 31:25 says, "laugh at the days to come" (NIV) because we know no hardship we face is a match for our God.

Scripture has a similar saying to Uncle Ben's: "From everyone who has been given much, much will be required" (Luke 12:48). While there are certainly things beyond our control that we cannot make happen on our own, there is a lot that can be done when we claim our rightful place as heirs of Christ and start taking God at His holy Word. If you have been given eternal life, much is required of you. But isn't this what

> *You have great power. You have great responsibility. You also have a great destiny.*

you have been secretly longing for all along? You have great power. You have great responsibility. You also have a great destiny.

We may sense the Holy Spirit nudging us to call a friend, a parent, or an estranged child. But then the thought comes to us, *No, I'm not going to do that. I'm just going to pray about it.* Here's the problem with that: passivity is not spirituality. We have an active God, not a passive God. There is nothing spiritual about not doing what we need to do. There is nothing spiritual about neglecting to mend relationships that need to be mended. There is nothing spiritual about refusing to see doctors who can heal us or our children.

Passivity is not spiritual; it's detrimental, whether the excuse is, "I'm not going to see a fertility doctor; I'm just going to pray about it," or "I'm not going to take my child who is struggling with depression to a counselor; I'm just going to pray about it," or "I'm not going to seek advice for my failing marriage; I'm just going to pray about it."

It's important to note that, while God has the power to do anything in anyone in any way He pleases, He often uses other people to accomplish His purposes. Doctors are not mutually exclusive from God's plan. God didn't look up one day and go, "Oh, no! Where did doctors come from? And how did counselors get on the planet?"

God has worked through the guidance and counsel of professionals at two of the most pivotal times in my life. The first time was when I was a college student and had a Christian counselor who spoke God's truth to me and helped me get to the point of rededicating my life to Christ and stepping off the road of rebellion that was certain to destroy me. The second time was when it became clear after three miscarriages that Ryan and I needed to see a fertility doctor who had the special training necessary to figure out what was going on.

Of course, this does not mean every doctor and every counselor is ordained by God to fix your every need. However, we are told time and again in the Bible to seek wise counsel. Proverbs 15:22 says, "Plans fail for lack of counsel, but with many advisers they succeed" (NIV). I don't know about you, but I don't want my plans to fail; I want them to succeed. So that means I need to seek the counsel of people who have the education and the spiritual background to help me, and then I need to actually do something. Plans that are not carried out are called wishes.

Ryan and I had to decide what to do about seeking fertility treatment. Finally, we decided to see a specialist. I'll always remember my first trip to the fertility doctor. My husband and I sat awkwardly in a waiting room, listening to the Backstreet Boys' greatest hits through the ceiling speaker while avoiding eye contact with other couples and commenting on the unusual art: a mermaid family statue. I'm not kidding. The sculpture was of a mommy and daddy mermaid holding a baby mermaid up in the air!

The artwork and music choice created a nice comedic relief from the anxiety of wondering what the doctor would say. What would be my prognosis? What if she said I had no chances of carrying a baby to term? What if there were no answers for why I easily became pregnant but could never stay pregnant? The roller coaster of three pregnancies followed by three miscarriages was a ride we were ready to get off.

The nurse eventually called us back to a consultation room that had all the posters and props of a high school health class, where we nervously played on our phones until the doctor finally came into the room. She sat down, looked through my medical history paperwork, and in no more than five minutes told us what she thought was wrong and how she planned to fix it. She confidently assured us she was not worried about my eventually carrying full-term. We left the doctor's office feeling very assured and encouraged.

I took a combination of fertility medications, including nightly shots Ryan gave me that were supposed to help with ovulation. We were cautiously optimistic about having multiples, though the doctor had said that twins would be extremely rare, with only a 6 to 12 percent chance. And triplets never even entered the conversation.

As Ryan and I proceeded with the fertility treatments, despite what the doctor said, and despite the fact that the odds seemed stacked against us, we continued to pray for multiples. We continued to pray for three biological children. And we also continued to pray for God to do "immeasurably more than all we ask or imagine" (Eph. 3:20 NIV).

Our triplets were conceived six months later. God answered our heartfelt prayers through the wisdom and the skill of doctors. He chose to use medication to help bring about our desire for a family, and maybe He wants to do the same in your life.

The Balance of Prayer and Action

Almost as soon as we got the miraculous news and announced we were having triplets, the questions began. At first, we were hesitant to tell people we had seen a fertility specialist, not because we were ashamed but because we didn't want anyone to discount the miracle God had worked in our lives. But even though we sought treatment, does that make three lives any less a miracle? God is either the creator of life or He isn't. There is nothing less miraculous about God working through science, medicine, or a memory lapse in taking birth control than carefully timed family planning. After three miscarriages, we decided to see specific doctors, and we encourage anyone going through that heartache to consider doing so as well. We conceived triplets because God ordained their lives and answered our specific prayers.

I remember having a pastor's wife reach out to me and ask how we had reconciled going to the fertility doctor with the Bible verse that says, "God opens and closes the womb." First of all, that is not an actual verse in the Bible. Isaiah 66:9 and Genesis 29:31, as well as other verses, give examples of God choosing to open and close the wombs of specific women and give credit to God for the creation of every life. Psalm 139:13–16 tells of the intimate way God knows us from the very beginning of our lives:

> For you formed my inward parts;
> You wove me in my mother's womb.
> I will give thanks to You, for I am fearfully and won-
>   derfully made;
> Wonderful are Your works,
> And my soul knows it very well.
> My frame was not hidden from You,
> When I was made in secret,
> And skillfully wrought in the depths of the earth;
> Your eyes have seen my unformed substance;
> And in Your book were all written
> The days that were ordained for me,
> When as yet there was not one of them.

God has ordained every day of our lives, but we should still wear seatbelts. The connection between our actions and God's sovereign plan may remain a mystery this side of heaven, but we cannot dismiss the reality that God works through our choices, wise counsel, and common sense. Medicine never limits God. God is more powerful than an antidepressant, a fertility drug, or a seatbelt. But for whatever reason, God uses these medications and precautions to help us. We are only hurting ourselves when we don't use these tools offered to us who are blessed to live in the twenty-first century.

If God has not ordained a life to be born, no amount of fertility drugs, herbal teas, or tricks you learned from your sister will matter at all. No baby is born outside God's will. No fertility medication works outside God's will. Fertility treatments don't bypass the God of all creation, of whom Job said, "I know that You can do all things, and that no purpose of Yours can be thwarted" (Job 42:2).

However, fertility medication is without a doubt a gray area in the Bible. God has not specifically said yes or no about this issue. What was right for us may not be right for you, and that is okay. Sometimes God tells us that something is not for us, and we need to wait for His green light before moving forward. Sometimes, as the old saying goes, "When plain sense makes good sense, seek no other sense, or it becomes nonsense." If you have a child who won't go to school because of anxiety issues, they most likely need to see a therapist. If you have been trying to get pregnant for ten years and still haven't, you most likely need to see a fertility specialist.

Action is not dismissing God's power; action is being an active part of His plan. There is a balance between the responsibility of prayer and action.

Praying in Faith with Power

Have you ever known people who have a deep relationship with God made obvious by the way they pray? When they are asked to pray publicly, you get a small glimpse into their closeness with God. Just being in the presence of hearing them pray seems like a high honor. (These are also the people I usually secretly hope I don't have to follow during a prayer time.) When they pray, these people bring down the house and all of our spiritual doubts with it! I love being prayed over by people like this. They pray as if they believe what they are praying about will happen and the God they are praying to will actually answer.

Excuses: whether they are from clients who are reluctant to talk about their hard issues, teenagers who put off doing their homework, or adults who seem to never make that appointment with the doctor, they remain the same: "I'll do it when I feel like doing it." "I don't feel like forgiving." "I don't feel like working out." "I don't feel like calling the doctor." The truth is that we probably will never wake up and want to do hard things. We are most likely not going to jump out of bed excited to mend broken relationships, confess our sin, or take the next steps toward addressing health concerns. The old axiom remains true: we don't feel our way into an action; we act our way into a feeling. With the rare exception, the action is first and the feeling follows. This is why a workout regimen or a Bible reading plan is so hard to begin but gets easier once we have done it for a consistent amount of time.

In my early twenties, I decided to read a verse or chapter in the Bible every day for a year. I wanted to see how my life would change if I woke up every day and heard from God before I heard from anyone else. Starting this habit was hard at first. I had many times I wanted to play on my phone, sleep in, or basically do anything other than my daily Bible reading. But as time went by and I consistently spent thirty, forty, and more days in God's Word, doing anything else in the morning started to become impossible. I acted my way into a feeling, and as a result, I experienced God like never before.

Joseph—An Example of Prayer in Action

Joseph did not romanticize or spiritualize his prison. On the contrary, Joseph actively tried to get out of prison any and every chance he was given.

We see this after Joseph interpreted the dreams of the cupbearer and the baker. He used his God-given gift of interpreting dreams not only to bring glory to God, to keep working, and to gain favor with others but also to keep the ball rolling. When he interpreted these two influencers' dreams, Joseph said, "Only keep me in mind when it goes well with you, and please do me a kindness by mentioning me to Pharaoh and get me out of this house" (Gen. 40:14). However, "the chief cupbearer did not remember Joseph, but forgot him" (v. 23).

My heart sinks when I read that verse. The sense of being forgotten is relatable and universal for all of us. Believing we have been forgotten is such a powerful tool of Satan. When I read this verse, I want to yell, "Joseph, you weren't forgotten! Don't worry! Chapter 41 is coming!" Of course, Joseph did not know that Genesis 41 existed, that his story would be chronicled in the bestselling book of all time, or even that he would live to see another day. But in the back of his mind, while trying to fall asleep in the midst of a foreign land, perhaps he held on to the fading memory of his God-given dream that seemed a lifetime away. The dream that was the source of his brothers' hatred, the dream that led to his abandonment by his family, the dream that led to his kidnapping, the dream that led to his imprisonment, the dream that ultimately would cause all of these things to work together for his good and the good of his whole people. The dream kept Joseph moving and kept reminding him that his current state was not his forever sentence. He had been promised more, and he was going to do everything in his power to experience more.

Joseph had faith that God would fulfill the dreams He had given him, and he kept acting accordingly by refusing to be a victim and actively believing God to be good, sovereign, and in control.

Too often we stay in our prison cells by our own admission. We stay too long in a place when God has created an escape. None of us will escape this life without trials and tribulation, but the very nature of trials is that they are not permanent. They are only for a season. There is a balance of fulfilling our purpose in a place, situation, or trial while at the same time keeping a lookout for how God may be working to move us from that place.

I am fascinated by how Joseph acted during his time in prison because it is so different from how most of us spend time in a place we don't want to be. The Bible never records Joseph complaining or falling into despair. Why does this matter? Because it shows that he stayed focused and faithful. Complaining doesn't honor God. Complacency doesn't honor God.

Christians are still allowed to be human. We are allowed to feel sadness, hurt, loneliness, anger—the whole realm of emotions. We also should have a different perspective that helps us see the truth and purpose in the midst of situations that threaten to break us. Jesus reminds us in John 16:33, "In the world you have tribulation, but take courage; I have overcome the world." We can overcome anything with the One who defeated death on our side.

Questions to Consider

The most influential people in the Bible were not passive. With God's divine power, they parted the seas, took on armies as teenagers, and even rose from the dead. However, sometimes we aren't sure what action we need to take in order to get our prayers answered and dreams fulfilled. In those circumstances, we need to ask two specific questions. First, does God's Word specifically address an issue? If not, does God's Word have principles that guide us in addressing it?

Does God's Word Specifically Address This Issue?

The Bible has much to say about many subjects. It's humbling to know that we are responsible for knowing not only the parts of the Bible we already have read but all of it. Whether we know the Scriptures or not is on us. Some questions are clearly answered in Scripture. For example, Christians don't have to wonder if they are supposed to marry a non-Christian. The Bible says in 2 Corinthians 6:14, "Do not be bound together with unbelievers." Christians don't have to pray about whether they should have sex before they are married or whether to cheat on their spouses. Hebrews 13:4 says, "Let marriage be held in honor among all, and let the marriage bed be undefiled, for God will judge the sexually immoral and adulterous" (ESV).

God never tells us to do anything that contradicts His Word. If the issue in question is already addressed in the Bible, then that is the standard.

Does God's Word Have Principles That Guide Us in Addressing This Issue?

However, not every decision we need to make has a corresponding Bible verse. For example, the book of Ephesians won't tell you which electrician to hire. The book of Hebrews won't tell you what college to attend. This is frustrating for some people but freeing for others. God knows when we need specific direction compared to when we need guiding principles.

A clear example of this is in the case of dating. The Bible says we aren't supposed to marry nonbelievers and we are to abstain from sexual immorality. Other than that, who are we to date? The Bible may not specifically answer your question, but guiding principles are readily available when we search for them: "Honor your father and mother" (Eph. 6:2). "Bad company corrupts good morals" (1 Cor. 15:33). "Reject every kind of evil" (1 Thess. 5:22 NIV).

Take Action

What are some other things we can do when we aren't sure what action we need to take in order to get our prayers answered and our dreams fulfilled?

85

Seek Wise Counsel

The Bible is clear that we are to seek wise counsel. We were never meant to live this life on our own (thank goodness!). God gives us a built-in support system: the local church. Fellow Christians are called our spiritual family, and often they are even closer to us than our biological family. We find counsel, encouragement, and safety in the family of God.

Unfortunately, sometimes in church we also can find people giving their opinion instead of God's opinion. This is something we are all guilty of, because we are all human. Some of the nicest people give the worst advice. Some well-meaning Christians give counsel from experience rather than from the Holy Spirit. Remember that the advice, counsel, or opinion of a Christian is not necessarily the advice, counsel, or opinion of God.

Listen to the Holy Spirit

There have been many times I have felt strongly that I should do something without having a specific Bible verse to back up my feelings. Remember, God will never tell you to do something that contradicts His Word. But He may tell you to do something, or not to do something, that isn't specifically found in a scriptural command. For example, no matter where you look in the Bible, there is not a verse that tells you which college to attend.

James 4:17 sheds light on how God speaks to our consciences individually to help us get to where we need to go: "Whoever knows the right thing to do and fails to do it, for him it is sin" (ESV). Sometimes it doesn't make sense why we feel convicted about a television show, song, substance, or relationship. Maybe the thing in and of itself isn't wrong or sinful. Maybe everyone you know is engaged in this activity, but in your spirit, you keep hearing a still, small voice telling you, *This isn't for you.*

Listen to that voice, if it doesn't contradict Scripture. And then see if you find the peace and unmistakable joy of a clear conscience.

Use Common Sense

We do not have to fast for forty days, go through the latest podcast series, or take a vow of silence until we hear from God. God speaks to us through the common sense He gave as part of the design of our minds. Merriam-Webster defines common sense as "sound and prudent judgment based on a simple perception of the situation or facts."[2] If you haven't conceived after ten years of trying to have a child, you probably need to see a doctor. If you can't get out of bed in the morning due to depression, you probably need to see a psychiatrist. If your parent is an alcoholic, you probably shouldn't drink alcohol. Some decisions require prayer, fasting, and time. Others are common sense.

> *Some decisions require prayer, fasting, and time. Others are common sense.*

Keep the Faith

During the year that Ryan and I suffered three miscarriages and sought medical help, I had many people tell me to "keep the faith." The sentiment was well-intended but also pretty vague. Who or what was I supposed to put my faith in, and exactly how was I to keep it?

It's interesting how we have the tendency to encourage people to keep going without directing them to the only One who actually can keep them going. It's also interesting how many people who don't know God still know that the survival of the human spirit is rooted in the charge to keep going and to believe there is more to this life than what we are presently experiencing. Faith is only as good as its object. We can have faith all day long that a chair will hold us up if we sit in it, but if its leg is broken, we'll fall. It doesn't matter how much faith we have if the object of our faith is not worthy or dependable. But if our faith is in the God of the Bible, who tells us, "Never will I leave you; never will I forsake you" (Heb. 13:5 NIV), we are in safe hands.

Prayer with Action

Every once in a while, we are blessed to cross paths with people who change us forever. One of these people for me is a client of mine who decided that she wanted to heal from the childhood sexual abuse inflicted by her uncle. She was constantly torn between false guilt, forgiveness, and moving forward in their relationship. She also was conflicted because she was a professing Christian while her uncle did not claim to know Christ. Where was the boundary line between the offender and the abused? What was the responsibility for someone who knows God's redemptive power and someone who does not?

Counselors are not supposed to tell clients what to do. We are taught to help guide people into figuring out what they need to do themselves. Sometimes I'm on the edge of my seat, knowing what decision the client should make, while other times I really don't know. For months, I worked with this woman through her healing from sexual abuse. But when she and I weren't working through the abuse, our conversation would always turn to her concern about her uncle's salvation. My counseling training tells me not to expose her to her abuser again. My biblical training tells me we are to tell everyone we can about Christ but also that it's okay to "go out of that house or that city [and] shake the dust off your feet" (Matt. 10:14) when people are unresponsive to our witness. I truly didn't know what she should do, and she didn't either. She was praying constantly for guidance to know what she should do.

During this time, a job opened up for me in full-time ministry, and I was ending sessions with my current clients. My last day of working at the clinic, I decided to listen to my voicemail one last time. The message was from this client, who said, "Julia, I've heard you are leaving, but I wanted you to know that I have decided to go to Indiana to witness to my uncle on his deathbed. I don't know if he will accept Christ or not, but I'm going to do my part to make sure he hears about Jesus."

We must pray, but we also must act.

Instead of only praying about what she should do, she also acted on Scripture. We must pray, but we also must act.

5

When God Says Yes

Prayer is the difference between the best we can do and
the best God can do.

                                        Mark Batterson

I don't want to scare you, but you're having triplets!" is a
sentence I will remember as long as I live. We were going
in for my first sonogram after getting a positive pregnancy
test. Our doctor performed the test in about two seconds
before telling us the news.

I started celebrating as if I had won an Olympic gold
medal—pumping my arms and cheering, thanking God, and
giving Ryan a majorly corny high five, though it took Ryan
a second to switch mindsets after hearing "I don't want to
scare you . . ." to comprehending this was the best news of
our lives. We were thrilled! It was the moment we knew our
prayers had been answered. It was the moment that changed
everything.

But was it really that moment, or was it the hundreds, if not thousands, of moments leading up to this moment that made the difference? This was the moment we found out our prayers were answered, but this was not the moment of God's actual intervention. This was merely the unveiling at the end of a building project. This was the diploma at the end of an educational endeavor. This was the prize at the end of an exhausting race. This was the moment we knew God had heard, seen, and been in all the other moments when we had been praying for big things.

We had asked, pleaded, and begged God for this very specific prayer request, and He answered as only the God of the universe can answer: timely, specifically, and powerfully. Our doctors and countless people since then have asked, "Were you surprised?" We always respond, "No, we weren't surprised, because we asked God and truly believed He would answer yes."

The Fear of What If?

While announcing the triplets to our student ministry, church family, and social media world was a blast, after three miscarriages in a year it was hard to ignore the deep-seated fear of What if? What if God doesn't let these babies live? What if we announce the triplets as this incredible miracle and then lose them like we lost the others? What if we announce the triplets to our student ministry but then have to provide grief counseling for three hundred–plus students? If something happens, does that mean God isn't good? If something happens, does that mean the triplets weren't miracles? If something happens, will we stop following God?

No, it wouldn't mean any of this because God is good, even if any of these things did happen. As my dad often says, "Faith is not believing God will do what we want Him to do. Faith is believing God is who He says He is and acting accordingly." God's goodness does not depend on whether we get what we want; God's goodness is the very nature of who God is and encompasses all He does, regardless of whether we understand or agree.

> *God's goodness does not depend on whether we get what we want.*

During the early part of the preg-nancy, I kept feeling a need to protect God. I would constantly remind every-one around me that God was good and in control no matter what happened. While this was true, it was more impor-tant for me to have human reactions than to be the resident theologian. My constant quotation of "God is good, even if . . ." combined with my paralyzing anxiety of not being able to even say the word *triplets* without fear washing over me like a tsunami to create an uncomfortable but necessary dichotomy. This conflict represented the balance of correct theology and the essence of being human. The importance of my claiming God is good no matter what was paramount to my not crumbling in fear. Coming to God with my fears, questions, and anxiety was equally important, as it allowed me to stay close to God and in touch with myself.

I started praying Psalm 30:9: "What is gained if I am si-lenced, if I go down to the pit? Will the dust praise you? Will it proclaim your faithfulness?" (NIV). I'm going to go out on a limb here and say this is probably no one's favorite Bible verse. But it represented the rawest truth I was experiencing. I committed that I would tell God over and over that I would follow Him no matter what—but I also reminded Him that with thousands of Christians praying, this would be a great win for the team. I told God that there really wasn't anything praiseworthy about letting the babies die and nothing would be gained if their lives were lost.

God's plan includes suffering, it includes circumstances that are beyond our understanding, and it even includes death. But this doesn't mean we aren't supposed to ask with everything in us for God to be our "very present help in trouble" (46:1).

As I look back on that time period, I honestly miss it. I never would want to go back to the uncertainty, but I miss having no option but to fully and totally trust God during my pregnancy, begging God to remember me and my children.

The Key to God's Blessings

How do we receive God's blessings? How do we live a life that truly matters? How do we have the Almighty God act mightily in our lives? What is the balance between our actions and God's blessings? I'm glad you asked! Before answering these questions, let's start with one fundamental truth: God does not owe us anything, but He has promised us everything. Our existence on earth may look very different from the eternal rewards in our ultimate home in heaven.

God does not owe us anything, but He has promised us everything.

In the Gospel of Matthew, Jesus tells us, "The last shall be first, and the first last" (20:16). We are all playing by the same rules. God has marked out how we are to live and has told us how He will act when we follow Him. Being obedient doesn't mean things always go as we planned, hoped, or prayed. Obedience puts us in the place of being able to receive God's blessings instead of His discipline. And that is a great place to be. Obedience unleashes God's blessing in our lives. Obedience is the key to God's blessings.

A few years ago, Ryan and I went to a Dave Ramsey seminar where Dave talked about the Jewish ritual of Havdalah. In this weekly custom, Jews fill the cup until it overflows as they ask God to pour out blessings on their family. Now, I come from a theological background that is very sensitive about not preaching anything remotely resembling the prosperity gospel, which, in a nutshell, is the belief Christians are entitled to a certain lifestyle here on earth. In this view, Christians should never get sick unless something is wrong spiritually. Their family life should go well unless they have done something wrong. Their lifelong battle with depression will be lifted if only they would give 70 percent of their earnings to the church.

Let me be clear that I do not believe in the prosperity gospel. I do not think we can force God's hand, and I do not agree that God "owes" us any material things. However, I do believe that God blesses those who are obedient to Him. So Ryan and I began praying, "Lord, pour out Your blessings on us." We unashamedly asked God to please bless us in any and every way possible—financially, relationally, spiritually, and physically.

Obedience is not a guarantee you will receive a million-dollar inheritance, your loved one will be healed, or your spouse will change. Obedience ensures that God takes notice of us, our lives and our faithfulness, and puts us in the place of receiving His blessing—whatever that may be. Sometimes peace in the midst of a storm is a bigger blessing than resolving the storm.

Psalm 18 describes how God intervenes in the lives of those who cry out to Him:

> In my distress I called upon the LORD
> And cried to my God for help;
> He heard my voice out of His temple,
> And my cry for help before Him came into His ears.
>
> Then the earth shook and quaked;
> And the foundations of the mountains were
> trembling
> And were shaken, because He was angry.
> Smoke went up out of His nostrils,
> And fire from His mouth devoured;
> Coals were kindled by it.
> He bowed the heavens also, and came down
> With thick darkness under His feet.
> He rode upon a cherub and flew;
> And He sped upon the wings of the wind. . . .
>
> He sent from on high, He took me;
> He drew me out of many waters.
> He delivered me from my strong enemy. . . .
> He rescued me, because He delighted in me.
>
> The LORD has rewarded me according to my righteousness. (Ps. 18:6–10, 16–17, 19–20)

Joseph—An Example of Obedience

Joseph did not wait to be invited, wait for others to see his dream-interpreting capabilities, or wait to be rescued by anyone. He made the most out of every opportunity to be noticed and remembered by others, with the goal of being rescued.

His constant faithfulness and obedience paid off when God gave him the green light. Joseph went all-in. He was called up to the plate, remembered his coach, and came to play.

> Then Pharaoh said to his servants, "Can we find a man like this, in whom is a divine spirit?" So Pharaoh said to Joseph, "Since God has informed you of all this, there is no one so discerning and wise as you are. You shall be over my house, and according to your command all my people shall do homage; only in the throne I will be greater than you." Pharaoh said to Joseph, "See I have set you over all the land of Egypt." . . .
>
> Thus Joseph stored up grain in great abundance like the sand of the sea, until he stopped measuring it, for it was beyond measure. (Gen. 41:38–41, 49)

I cannot help but smile upon reading the phrase, "for it was beyond measure." God longs to be gracious to us and to do things in our lives that are beyond measure, beyond our wildest dreams.

I imagine Joseph had fantasized about being rescued and released. I doubt he had dreamed of being Pharaoh's second in command, with no one being able to set foot in the land he was a captive in without his permission. But such is God, who promises, "No eye has seen, no ear has heard, and no mind has imagined what God has prepared for those who love him" (1 Cor. 2:9 NLT). Day after day, Joseph kept being faithful and obedient. God saw all of it and rewarded him accordingly.

Take Action

There is no way of knowing what God is preparing you for in the future. But isn't that part of the excitement? God wants us to keep being faithful. Keep obeying. Keep praying. The apostle Peter wrote, "Humble yourselves under the mighty hand of God, that He may exalt you at the proper time" (1 Pet. 5:6). How do we humble ourselves so that we can receive God's blessing?

Confess Any Known Sin

First, we can confess our sin. Habitual sin is different from an accidental sin. The root word *habit* is obviously in the word *habitual*. The picture of habitual sin is having a fist raised to God in the attitude of, "I know I'm sinning, but I just don't care and I'm not going to change!"

This kind of sin is the one we battle with, sometimes for years. This is the sin that often keeps us out of church, out of fellowship with other believers, and running for high ground when anything or anyone remotely spiritual threatens our way of life. This sin entraps us, kills us, and leads us further from God than we ever imagined. This is the sin that used to be so clearly sin before we looked up and saw it was no longer an action but a way of life.

We are to "put on the Lord Jesus Christ, and make no provision for the flesh in regard to its lusts" (Rom. 13:14). In other words, we are to make no way for sin to enter our lives. Sin is a deadly virus that threatens everything we ultimately want and everything God wants us to be. You will never fully unleash God's power in your life until you confess and repent of habitual sin. We place a limit on ourselves when we ignore the Holy Spirit.

I developed the habit a few years ago of recommitting my life to the Lord every morning. I wake up and say, "God, I'll do whatever You want me to do today. Show me what that is, and help me to do it!" We want to obey. We want to have a clear conscience. We want to unleash God's power and blessing in our lives.

Let me encourage you with something my sister told me yesterday on the phone: "Well, God hasn't been wrong so far." No, He sure hasn't, and He isn't going to start now. If God is tugging at your heart, then listen. If you think something is wrong but don't know what it is, ask God to reveal it to you through His Word. The Bible doesn't tell us what supermarket to go to but it does tell us how to have peace, how to date, how to have a successful marriage, how to find our life purpose, how to manage money, how to be wise, and the list goes on and on. We pave the way for God's blessings when we give up that sin that is hurting us. Remember, God longs to be gracious to us.

> *Remember, God longs to be gracious to us.*

Claim God's Word as Truth

Second, we can claim God's Word. My whole life changed when I quit seeing the Bible as a book of suggestions and instead started seeing it as the only way life would work. God's Word is true for everyone, not just for me, not just for missionaries, and not just for the spiritually elite. God's Word is true for you, my friend, and it has the power to change everything. The problem is that when we say "claim God's Word," most of us don't know what to claim because we really don't know what the Bible says. The Bible is not a collection of abstract ideas that we have to attend seminary in order to decipher.

To give you a taste of the practicality found in the Bible, here are just a few of the commands, promises, and instructions it has for us:

> If we are a follower of Jesus Christ, then we are chosen (Eph. 1:4–5).
>
> A lot of the things we don't have are the result of not asking God for them or asking with wrong motives (James 4:3).
>
> Divorce and remarriage are allowed when there is infidelity or desertion (Matt. 5:31–32; 1 Cor. 7:10–16).
>
> God promises to avenge wrongs and evildoing (Rom. 12:19).

Clear Your Conscience

Third, we can clear our conscience. When I was a little girl, I would come home every day after school and tell my parents everything I had done wrong that day. I would confess every bad intention, every unkind action, every sin big and little I had committed during my eight-hour day of elementary school. My parents had it pretty easy (at least for my elementary years) because I would just come home and tell on myself. Was I really that bad of a kid? No, but I had a disproportionate view of the Scripture verses "Confess your sins to one another, and pray for one another so that you may be healed" (James 5:16) and "Against You, You only, I have sinned" (Ps. 51:4). My parents thought it was cute at first but quickly saw how much distress that confessing every envious thought about hair bows was causing me.

It's often hard to know the difference between actual con-
viction, overanalyzing, and self-condemnation. Psychology
has a term for religious people who mercilessly analyze their
every action and thought, resulting in paralyzing anxiety:
scrupulosity. This is not where any of us thrive. This is not
God's desire for us.

Our culture tends to swing to the other extreme of no
accountability while holding the banner high of "Do not
judge, or you too will be judged" (Matt. 7:1 NIV). This
ignores the biblical command to flee from sin and to restore
people who are living a life of sin. Then sometimes we throw
in, "To one who knows the right thing to do and does not
do it, to him it is sin" (James 4:17), meaning that the gray
areas of life are okay for some people but may not be right
for you.

So, what are we to do? I love my dad's definition of a clear
conscience: "The knowledge that neither God nor anyone
else can accuse you of a wrong you have not attempted to
make right." God doesn't accuse Christians. We are forgiven
and in a right standing with Him from an eternal judgment
standpoint. Our sin is "forgiven, forgotten, forever" as the
church song goes. But there are times in our lives where our
parental relationship with God is in a difficult place because
of sin in our lives. God often wants the sin addressed before
He answers our heartfelt pleas. I encourage you to honestly
ask God to show you if there is anything in your life dis-
pleasing to Him. As far as overanalyzing our actions goes,
if the action isn't something that Jesus had to die for, it isn't
a sin. Simple as that. But if there is something that needs
to change, change it. Let us not get in the habit of ignoring
the Holy Spirit.

Commit to Obedience

Fourth, we obey to the best of our ability. When I hear *obedience*, I often think of a dog owner commanding her dog to sit. Honestly, that image is not too motivational as I think about how I am supposed to follow God. Obedience is not always exciting. Obedience is not always fun. Obedience is rarely easy. But obedience always gets God's attention.

Second Chronicles 16:9 tells us, "The eyes of the LORD run to and fro throughout the whole earth, to give strong support to those whose heart is blameless toward him" (ESV).

> Obedience is not always easy, but it is always worth it.

"To give strong support" is such an impactful phrase. I want God's strong support. The Alpha and Omega, the Beginning and the End, the God who was and is and is to come strongly supports those whose hearts are blameless toward Him. That seems like a winning combination to me.

Obedience is not always easy, but it is always worth it.

Depend on God to Keep His Promises

Fifth, we depend on God's trustworthiness. God is going to keep His Word. The apostle Paul wrote in 2 Timothy 2:13, "If we are faithless, He remains faithful, for He cannot deny Himself." Faithfulness is the essence of God's existence.

We are to concern ourselves with being obedient, making the most out of our opportunities, furthering the cause of Christ, and giving God the glory—and God will do the rest. "Do you see a man skilled in his work? He will stand before kings; he will not stand before obscure men" (Prov. 22:29). God sees your hard work. God sees your knee work. God sees your heart work. God sees and rewards accordingly. His timetable may not be our timetable, but God is never late, never early, and always on time.

"Quit Waiting for an Invitation to Your Own Life"

Sixth, we give all we have, and we give it now. I was once watching a television show in which a young woman blurted out to her mother, "Quit waiting for an invitation to your own life!" I think that is a brilliant line. How much time are we wasting waiting to be invited to our own lives? We wait for an invitation. We wait for a certain amount of income. We wait to see if we are accepted by others. We wait for God to lay out the whole plan before obeying.

> *We honor God when we give this life all we have.*

We wait around and let others live our lives. We wait. And as we wait, we waste opportunities, relationships, and time. We honor God when we give this life all we have.

Go All-In

When God gives the green light, we go all-in! We pray hard. We work hard. We do everything we can in our power to honor what God has blessed us with; to protect it, to make the most of it, to leave no rock unturned and no opportunity missed. We do all we can while we can, and depend on God to do what we cannot do.

Mark Batterson says in his book *Draw the Circle* to remember that we are always just one degree from knowing anyone, because God knows everyone.[1] This idea is what led to Ryan and me praying for a TV show when we had no connections whatsoever to a producer. We wanted to get the miraculous story of our triplets to as big of an audience as possible so that as many people as possible could be encouraged. We prayed that God would open that door, and He did. Our job was to pray big things, and God answered in big ways!

We honor God when we dream big, pray bigger, and give Him all we have. Dreaming big shows the faith we have in Him. Praying big shows the trust we have in Him. Giving God all we have shows our gratefulness for His blessings.

> *We honor God when we dream big, pray bigger, and give Him all we have.*

Luke 16:10 reminds us, "He who is faithful in a very little thing is faithful also in much; and he who is unrighteous in a very little thing is unrighteous also in much." Let us prove ourselves faithful with every little thing that we are given so that God is able to entrust us with even more because He knows He can count on us to be faithful.

6

Panic and Prayer Warriors

All our fret and worry is caused by calculating without God.

Oswald Chambers

Because then I'll end up in a one-room apartment surrounded by twelve cats and living off Ramen noodles! I'm going to be the weird cat lady, Julia! Is that what you want?" the sixteen-year-old sitting across from me exclaimed. This high school student doomed to be a cat lady was incredibly anxious, had difficulty eating and sleeping, and had very worried parents. She had been adopted and had a lot of questions about her biological parents. This is natural and normal for children who have been adopted, but it can be upsetting for their adoptive parents. After a few sessions, she eventually told me that she was worried about her grades—in particular, her English grade. To which I replied, "What is the worst that can happen?"

Shocked, she looked at me and exclaimed, "I thought you were supposed to *help* me with my anxiety! I can't think about what the worst is, or I'll be more anxious!"

I convinced her to trust my tactics and promised that if they didn't work, then we could do something different.

She conceded and said, "Well, if I don't get a good grade in English, then I'll fail eleventh grade. If I fail eleventh grade, then I'll be forever behind and could never catch up senior year. If I don't catch up senior year, then I won't be able to get into a good college. If I can't go to a good college, then I will just end up flipping burgers forever. If I just flip burgers, then I won't meet a nice guy to marry. If I don't meet a nice guy, then I'll probably never get married, and eventually I'll live in a one-room apartment surrounded by twelve cats and living off Ramen noodles!"

I replied, "Then what would you do?" She had a look of absolute absurdity on her face, as if I had asked her to move to the moon.

She replied, "Well, I guess I would be okay and figure out how to still be happy."

What If . . . ?

After the spiritual and emotional high of finding out about our miraculous triplet pregnancy came the overwhelming fear of miscarriage, stillbirth, and infant loss. I didn't sleep for nearly a month after being told I was pregnant with triplets. At first, I didn't sleep because I was so excited. I remember spending the entire first night we found out just looking at my stomach in the bathroom mirror in unbelief that it housed three little lives. Then I did not sleep because I was terrified. I even banned my family from saying the word *triplets* until the second trimester because it would send me into an anxiety attack.

Being pregnant with triplets seemed too good to be true. What if the babies didn't survive? What if only one or two of them survived? What if they came too early? What if they had one of the thousand complications that Google was telling me were possible for multiples? What if I didn't survive? What if we had no way to pay for everything they needed? What if . . . ?

In order for me to be able to function, my thought pattern had to change. I started asking myself a different set of What-ifs. What if I started living, thinking, and believing like the God who called me to this would see me through it? What if I started believing God and I were on the same team? What if I believed that God really loved me, really loved these babies, and really knew what He was doing?

Now was the moment I had been preparing for all my life. All the hours I spent in Bible drill classes, memorizing God's Word, all my time listening to sermons about God's faithfulness and power, all my life spent proclaiming the goodness of God had led to this moment, this challenge, this miracle. I chose to lean into God, and He chose to show me His power and peace like never before.

How Anxiety Affects Our Spiritual Life

"I don't feel God anymore." That is one of the most common complaints I hear from people who are struggling with depression and anxiety. But we don't have to have a clinical diagnosis in order to not sense God's presence. The consistent state of worry that many of us live in is enough to make us stop feeling connected to God. Anxiety is fear based on irrational thought.

While fear is a feeling that is associated with a real threat, anxiety comes from thinking about a perceived threat. In his book *Anatomy of the Soul*, Curt Thompson explains that the mind of a person struggling with anxiety and depression becomes disintegrated.[1] This means that our brain is not functioning as God designed it to function, and we have a harder time connecting with God. The left hemisphere of our brain is the analytical side. The right hemisphere of our brain is the emotional, feeling, trusting side. For whatever reason, many Christians seem to gravitate toward the left side of the brain—they are able to analyze, quote Scripture, and do spiritual rituals without the right side of the brain functioning properly. This is why they experience a sense of disconnect from God and talk about "not feeling God."

> *The consistent state of worry that many of us live in is enough to make us stop feeling connected to God.*

Both sides of our brain have to be functioning well in order to experience God the way that we are made to, and experience "the peace of God, which surpasses all comprehension" (Phil. 4:7). I've definitely had times when I don't feel God and have to rely on what I know instead of what I feel. David Benner, author of *The Gift of Being Yourself*, puts it this way: "Having information about God is no more transformational than having information about love."[2]

Anxiety robs us of joy. Anxiety takes away the creative, dreaming, emotional, trusting side of our lives, making it nearly impossible for us to pray big things.

Dealing with Anxiety

Anxiety and worry seem like little sins. It is hard to believe that something that goes on in the depths of our minds could be wrong. Perhaps it is so wrong because it is so detrimental. God knows how much anxiety and worry will harm us, and that is why He warns about them so much in His Word.

What causes anxiety? The simplest answer is negative self-talk. My postgraduate counseling supervisor, Dr. Keith Cobern, used to tell his students, "It is impossible to be anxious and be telling yourself the truth."

Let me pause here and say that there are very real anxiety disorders that can be diagnosed and treated with prescribed medication. However, *anyone* can make themselves anxious by catastrophizing, obsessing on negative thoughts, and/or lying to themselves.

How do we know if we are believing the truth or not? Telling yourself the truth is not repeating "I'm a princess and I'm going to live in a castle" over and over again until your fairy godmother shows up with an impressive gown made by singing animals, complete with a pumpkin carriage to the ball. Telling yourself the truth means telling yourself God's truth. You repeatedly and habitually cling to what God says is true about you and your situation.

My former boss, renowned psychiatrist Dr. Paul Meier, has said, "Medication can control anxiety, but only the truth can heal anxiety." One of my favorite truths about the Bible is that it is practical, relevant, and timeless. God never asks us in Scripture to do something we are not able to do with His help. There is no Bible verse that says, for instance, "Don't have cancer," because that is something beyond a person's control. There is no Bible verse that says, "Don't be born with blonde hair," because that would just be silly and also beyond a person's control. However, there are verses in the Bible that tell us not to be anxious, because that is within our control. With God's direction and help, we can be set free from anxiety.

With God's direction and help, we can be set free from anxiety.

As the classic Christian song claims, joy may be something that is meant to be "in our heart to stay," but more often joy is something that seems really far away. Joy belongs to us but has been robbed from many of us.

Joy is more than an ornately decorated word on the front of a Christmas card. Joy is more than happiness. The joy we are able to experience as Christians is meant to change everything about our lives. Paul talked about joy constantly while he was in prison, when he was shipwrecked, and as he was persecuted for the faith. Happiness is fleeting and depends on circumstances. Joy is forever and is untouchable by circumstances. Joy comes from knowing that "if God is for us, who is against us?" (Rom. 8:31). Joy comes from knowing that God is just and there is no evil in Him. Joy comes from having the assurance that no matter what happens in this life—abuse, abandonment, death—we will ultimately see Jesus face-to-face and spend eternity with Him in heaven.

A Joyful Perspective of Death

Knowing you have beaten death ultimately puts everything else in perspective.

My grandmother, Judy Jeffress, died very young and very quickly. She was diagnosed with terminal colon cancer at the age of fifty-four and passed away three months later. Because of her wide influence as a journalism teacher and her lifelong ministry to teenagers, the *Dallas Morning News* interviewed my grandmother on her deathbed. The journalist asked Judy, "What is it like to know you are dying?"

My quick-witted grandmother responded, "We are all dying. The difference is that some of us know it and others don't."

Judy's response could be heard as sad, scary, or wise, depending on each individual's interpretation and certainty of salvation. Judy was living the reality that, for Christians, what others see as the worst-case scenario we can see as the best-case scenario. As the apostle Paul says, "To live is Christ and to die is gain" (Phil. 1:21).

In her book *Mercy Triumphs*, Beth Moore encourages readers to focus on one part of James 4:15: "If the Lord wills, we will live." What a humbling sentence. If the Lord wills, we live through the end of the year, the end of the week, the end of the day. Teenagers love to ask, "If no one dies before God is ready for them to die, then why do I have to wear a seatbelt?" The easy answer is, "If you don't wear a seatbelt, then it is going to be your time to die very soon." However, that really isn't the theologically correct answer because the Bible is clear that our days have been ordained. In the wise words of Corrie ten Boom, "Never be afraid to trust an unknown future to a known God."[3] We don't know what the future holds, but we know the One who holds the future.

Fear and anxiety rob us of joy and truth.

Psalm 84:11 tells us, "For the LORD God is a sun and shield; the LORD gives grace and glory; no good thing does He withhold from those who walk uprightly."

Fear and anxiety rob us of joy and truth. God says to us, "Do not fear, for I have redeemed you; I have called you by name; you are Mine!" (Isa. 43:1). "Have I not commanded you? Be strong and courageous! Do not tremble or be dismayed, for the LORD your God is with you wherever you go" (Josh. 1:9).

Life Is Not about Us

I'll always remember the moment God shouted, through the Google search engine, that my life was not about me. After my first trimester of pregnancy had passed, I really thought I was in the clear and could finally enjoy the pregnancy. I arrived home after the two-week trip that marked the end of the first trimester, turned on my computer, and decided to Google "triplet moms." Man, was that a mistake. The first article to pop up was the story of a triplet mom who had passed away a few days after delivering triplets, leaving behind her husband, four-year-old son, and triplet newborn girls. I was crushed. I was angry. I was shocked.

Then two thoughts rushed over me like a tsunami as I sat down to gain my balance: First, my babies were not my own. And second, God could decide to call me home anytime He chose.

It was the moment I realized that my life was not about me. It was the moment I realized that regardless of how many specialists we saw, how many prenatal vitamins and special medications I took, how much I prayed and read Scripture, I wasn't in control. This revelation was crippling for a moment but freeing in the long months ahead.

If the babies weren't really mine and my life wasn't really mine, then I really didn't gain anything by worrying, and I'd better start living. But I couldn't start living because I was so scared. "Start living" was not the correct solution. I had to start *surrendering*. I didn't have another choice.

Since God's Word says He is responsible for my life, I decided to give over the reins and let Him be responsible. Not that He needed my permission, but I needed to decide in my heart that my story was not my story, my triplet story was not my triplet story, and my life was not my life.

I am here for one purpose: to tell others about Christ. And I will do the most I can to tell others about Christ until God decides my time on this earth is over.

Boldly Approach the Throne of Grace

At the end of my first trimester, Ryan and I went on our annual vacation and attempted to have our annual prayer walk. I was exhausted all the time, so instead of walking, we opted to sit outside on the balcony of our hotel room. The day was cloudy and rainy as we began our prayer time. I was so distraught, anxious, and fearful about the pregnancy that I decided I was going to pray with boldness like never before.

As I prayed, I told God that it was His job to take care of these babies. I prayed with certainty, closeness, and confidence to approach "the throne of grace . . . [to] receive mercy and find grace to help in time of need" (Heb. 4:16). I told God that people were watching what He was going to do with these three lives, so His reputation was involved. People knew we were believers, they knew we had put our faith and trust in Him, and it was His job to take care of us. I declared that God was good no matter what, but that the triplets' birth would be an amazing win for believers who had heard the story.

I was overcome with angst and heart-wrenching fear as I called on the name of the Lord. Then I felt the sun shining directly on my face, as if God had parted the clouds. I opened my eyes because I couldn't believe it was happening, nudged Ryan so he could see it too, and then we just smiled. In that moment, I knew we were going to be okay because God was our "sun and shield" (Ps. 84:11).

Confront Satan's Lies with God's Truth

Why don't we trust God? Satan has been lying to us and tempting us to doubt God since day one in the garden with Eve, and his tactic has not changed: "Indeed, has God said . . . ?" (Gen. 3:1).

The Genesis account of Satan leading Eve into sin serves as a blueprint to Satan's tactics with all of us. The trap he used for Eve is the same trap laid for us today, based on three main lies.

Lie #1: God Isn't Good

You may be hard-pressed to find someone who will publicly raise their hand to declare "God is not good," especially if you live in the Bible Belt, as I do. Yet countless people secretly think, believe, question, and ultimately let their doubt of God's goodness shape their faith and future. This is a lie Satan has been spinning from the beginning of time in the garden with Eve: *God really doesn't have your best interest in mind. God is withholding good from you.*

But the Bible repeatedly declares that "the LORD is good" (Ps. 34:8). Goodness is the very definition of who He is and how He acts toward humanity. Psalm 107:1 says, "Give thanks to the LORD, for He is good, for His lovingkindness is everlasting." And in Psalm 145:9, the psalmist says, "The LORD is good to all, and His mercies are over all His works."

So often we relate to God much like a toddler throwing a tantrum and yelling, "Why?" after being told they can't do something. We think He is an unfair parent while really He is our loving heavenly Father who sees the whole picture. Eating from the tree of the knowledge of good and evil really did cause sin to enter the world, Eve's children to kill one another, childbirth to be painful, and ultimately people to go to hell. So, yes, God was being truthful, fair, loving, and good when He said, "From any tree of the garden you may eat freely; but from the tree of the knowledge of good and evil you shall not eat" (Gen. 2:16–17).

Lie #2: God Doesn't Care about Our Dreams

Eve wanted to be like God. Genesis 3:6 reveals Eve's motivation for sinning against the Lord: "When the woman saw that the tree was good for food, and that it was a delight to the eyes, and that the tree was desirable to make *one* wise, she took from its fruit and ate."

When we get to the root of most of our sin and acting out, we can see we also want to be like God. We want to be in control. We think we know everything. We have big plans, and we think that if we can manipulate God just right, He may let these dreams come true.

When we want what He wants for ourselves and the world, then God honors our desires.

The truth is that God gave us our dreams and aspirations. Psalm 37:4 says, "Delight yourself in the LORD; and He will give you the desires of your heart." When we delight ourselves in the Lord, then our ultimate desire is God. And when we want what He wants for ourselves and the world, then God honors our desires.

Lie #3: God Isn't Interested in What I Want

Satan spun the lie that God and Eve wanted different things. Eve believed that in order to be happy, successful, powerful, and content, she had to go outside of God's will to make it happen. Eve believed she had to separate her desires from her God. Yet God is the One who created marriage, friendship, family, work, church, and everything else on earth, which means He knows how it will work best.

Joseph—An Example of Trusting God

It would have been scary to know that seven years of famine were on the way. However, Joseph did not live with a *What if?* mindset. We have no scriptural documentation of Joseph asking himself, *What if I interpreted the dream wrong? What if there really isn't going to be a famine? What if Potiphar decides he doesn't want a follower of the Lord as his right-hand man after all? What if I'm not qualified to rule as second in command of Egypt?*

Now, there is no record of Joseph thinking this way, but we know the temptation to think What if? thoughts was likely something he experienced. How do we know this? While Joseph is a hero of the faith, he was also human. Remember Satan's tactic with Eve: "Indeed, has God said . . . ?" which leads to the follow-up question, "Can God really be trusted?"

What we know for certain is that whatever mind games or temptations he experienced, Joseph pushed past them and focused on the God who called him and sustained him. Joseph lived as if God had been preparing him all his life for this. He didn't live in fear; he lived in faith. God had been preparing Joseph since he was a child for the greatest trial, test, and ultimate triumph of his life.

Joseph became second in command of Egypt, saved an entire country, and ultimately forgave his brothers. These, of course, are amazing accomplishments. However, I think Joseph's faithfulness to God in the midst of abandonment, loneliness, isolation, kidnapping, slavery, and imprisonment is his most impressive accomplishment. His relentless resolve to keep going, to not give up, to refuse to let others break him, and to keep trusting God are what make him a hero of the faith. When we live with that kind of fearlessness and faithfulness, we experience God's provision and promises like never before.

Take Action

So many of our mental battles originate with the thought, *Can God really be trusted?* We think things like, *Can I really trust God with the outcome of this surgery? Can I really trust God to answer this prayer request with my best in mind? Can I really trust God with this relationship? Can I really trust God with my future?*

Let's look at four things we can do to trust God when we are feeling anxious.

Live with Joy Instead of What-If

One, we can live with joy instead of being stuck in the mind game of What if?, which can keep us absolutely paralyzed. Constantly thinking, analyzing, and obsessing over What if? possibilities strangles our hope and robs our joy. In order to be robbed of something, that something must belong to us. Joy belongs to us if we have put our hope and trust in Christ.

Joy is a birthright of every born-again Christian. We are joyful because, ultimately, we have put our hope and faith in the Lord Jesus Christ who has defeated death. Because He defeated death, we have defeated death and get to live in heaven for all eternity.

Take Courage and Work Hard

Two, we can harness the power of courage and hard work. In Haggai 2, as God's people were allowed to return to their land after many years in exile, a man named Zerubbabel was given the monumental task of overseeing the rebuilding of the temple in Jerusalem. The returning exiles were discouraged at the meager construction, which fell far short of the temple's former glory. *What if we can't finish building the temple? What if this temple isn't as good as the previous one?* The Lord acknowledged their concerns and What if? thoughts. He said to the people, "Who is left among you who saw this temple in its former glory? And how do you see it now? Does it not seem to you like nothing in comparison?" (v. 3). Then the Lord said to Zerubbabel, "Take courage . . . and work; for I am with you" (v. 4).

What task are you facing right now that seems insurmountable? What circumstance or struggle is causing you to feel discouraged? God's words of assurance to Zerubbabel are the same message He has for you and for me: take courage and work, for God is with you. Open your eyes to the magnificent plans God has in store for you!

Lean into God; Don't Run from God

Three, we can choose to lean into God instead of running from Him. What are some of the lies you are telling yourself that make you run from God instead of to Him? Do you think He is angry with you? God's Word assures us, "The LORD is gracious and merciful; slow to anger and great in loving-kindness" (Ps. 145:8). Do you think you have sinned so much that God can no longer use you? Scripture says, "Our great God and Savior, Christ Jesus . . . gave Himself for us to redeem us from *every lawless deed*, and to purify for Himself a people for His own possession, zealous for good deeds" (Titus 2:13–14). Do you think your circumstances prevent you from experiencing God's love? The Bible is clear: "I am convinced that neither death, nor life, nor angels, nor principalities, nor things present, nor things to come, nor powers, nor height, nor depth, nor any other created thing, will be able to separate us from the love of God, which is in Christ Jesus our Lord" (Rom. 8:38–39).

When you are tempted to run from God, lean into Him instead. Even if your faith is very small—the size of a mustard seed (Matt. 17:20)—Jesus said,

> *When you are tempted to run from God, lean into Him instead.*

"All things are possible to him who believes" (Mark 9:23). I urge you to come to Jesus and be completely honest about your fears, your doubts, and your concerns. And you can cry out, along with the father of a boy who was healed by Jesus, "I do believe; help my unbelief" (v. 24).

Remember It's Not about You; It's All about Him

Four, we can remember that it is about God, not us. We are not responsible for the outcome of things we have no control over. What we are responsible for is praying like it depends on God and working like it depends on us. Ultimately, whatever the circumstance may be, God is responsible for the outcome that furthers His purpose. As much as we can want something with all our heart and pray for it with all our might, if the request isn't in God's good and perfect plan, then it's not the plan for us. Opening our hands to say *Not my will but thy will be done* is so hard but so freeing.

The Balance of Trusting God

At my first appointment with the doctor who would deliver the triplets, I asked, "At what point in the pregnancy will I be able to relax?"

He smiled and said, "At twelve weeks, you will be past the miscarriage point. At twenty-two weeks, you will be past the cervical incompetence point. At twenty-four weeks, your triplets will be viable. At twenty-eight weeks, the babies will have great odds of survival. But Julia, as a parent, there will always be something new to worry about."

I remember thinking that remark was a tad flippant considering my high-risk pregnancy and history of miscarriages. Now, over a year into life with triplets, I can see I will always have something I can worry about.

The same is true for all of us. There will always be a What if? waiting around the corner to pounce on us just when we are starting to enjoy our life. How about instead of going down that rabbit hole, we started acting, praying, believing, and experiencing life through the lens of "What if God really is for me?" What else matters at that point? Truly believing that God is for us frees us. There is a stark contrast in quality of life between people calculating risks just to walk across the sidewalk and those enjoying God's blessings. We decide what we think about—what we "water" in our minds. And what we water grows.

7

Purpose in the Pain

God never allows pain without a purpose in the lives
of His children. . . . God never wastes pain. He always
causes it to work together for our ultimate good, the
good of conforming us more to the likeness of His Son.

Jerry Bridges

After I was admitted to the hospital at twenty-three
weeks for preterm labor, the senior neonatologist solemnly told Ryan and me, "Your babies will likely be born
blind, deaf, severely disabled, and have brain bleeds if your
preterm labor continues." Contractions had begun, and fear
was lurking at the door to seize our hope and faith. I told
Ryan that he and the doctor had to leave my hospital room.
I truly felt like quoting Jesus's words to Peter in Matthew
16:23: "Get behind Me, Satan! You are a stumbling block
to Me; for you are not setting your mind on God's interests,
but man's."

Of course, the doctor was not Satan, any more than Peter was. He was just doing his job. However, the fear, doubt, and despair caused by that meeting was something my heart couldn't take. I was angered to my core with what I believe to be the Holy Spirit shouting, *No! This will not be so!* in my mind and heart as the doctor spoke.

Ryan stepped into the hallway with the doctor and listened to the rest of the heartbreaking prognosis for Blair, Barrett, and Blake. When he came back into my hospital room, we both looked at each other with sobering expressions, and almost at the same time said, "That isn't going to be their story." These children we had begged God to protect were now, in a blink of an eye, facing disability and possible death. What were we going to do?

What we thought was going to be a few days of observation in the hospital turned into a forty-nine-day hospital bedrest stay. With every day that passed, we would wake up and plead with God on behalf of our children. We would look at what medical complications threatened their lives if they were born that day. We would have breakfast together. Ryan would go to work, and I would read my Bible, pray, and try to figure out how to stay calm with the knowledge that at any moment our precious triplets could come too soon. I didn't know in those first few days that I would spend the next hours, days, weeks, and months staring out a single window, wondering what the future held. I also didn't know it would be the best experience of my life.

Faith in the Midst of Suffering

There is something truly special, sobering, and spiritual when you are not in control. Of course, none of us is ever truly in control of anything but only under the illusion of it. Our schedules, lists, New Year's resolutions, and ten-year plans support William Ernest Henley's promise in his famous poem "Invictus": "It matters not how strait the gate, how charged with punishments the scroll, I am the master of my fate: I am the captain of my soul."[1] But the idea that we are the ones ultimately controlling our lives is not true.

Occasionally we are faced with circumstances that make the abstract truth a harsh reality impossible to ignore. Being bound to a bed as an adult while others help you do tasks that you mastered as a five-year-old is a very humbling experience. Recently, before filming a TV interview, Ryan and I sat in the car prepping. I asked him what he thought was the main lesson he'd learned through our trials with infertility, miscarriages, and bedrest. He replied, "I learned that it is possible to still have a thriving relationship with God in the midst of suffering."

How do we stay close to God when He appears to have let us down? How do we trust His plan is good when it is nothing we would have chosen? How do we stay faithful when fear and doubt crouch at the door mocking our relationship with God and making childlike faith a distant memory? How do we have hope in the midst of heartbreak?

Hope in the Heartbreak

Joni Eareckson Tada was forever changed when she became a paraplegic at the young age of seventeen. She credits her horrific accident as being the main source of understanding the gospel she had accepted just three years before.

Although the gospel took root in my heart that night, something happened nearly 3 years later that threatened to undo everything. It occurred just a few weeks after my high school graduation when I went swimming in the Chesapeake Bay with my sister. I took a dive into what ended up being very shallow water. My head hit the bottom, it snapped my neck back, and my spinal cord was crushed. Immediately I was paralyzed. Oh, I sank into depression and, yes, the gospel was nearly uprooted, but thankfully, Christian friends were praying and these same friends carried me through some of the darkest, most difficult days of my life. And what I learned back then about the Lord Jesus and his fellowship of sufferings helped sink the roots of the gospel far deeper into my heart than I could've ever experienced had I not become paralyzed. And now, 50 years later, I still live to tell the story. My wheelchair, more than anything else, has become the theology textbook that has shown me so much about the sustaining grace of God.[2]

Joni certainly didn't have a hopeful perspective immediately. She recalls:

I was once the 17-year-old who retched at the thought of living life without a working body. I hated my paralysis so much I would drive my power wheelchair into walls, repeatedly banging them until they cracked. Early on, I found dark companions who helped me numb my depression with scotch-and-cola. I just wanted to disappear. I wanted to die. . . .

Back in the '70s, my Bible study friend Steve Estes shared ten little words that set the course for my life: "God permits what he hates to accomplish what he loves." Steve explained it this way: "Joni, God allows all sorts of things he doesn't approve of. God hated the torture, injustice, and treason that led to the crucifixion. Yet he permitted it so that the world's worst murder could become the world's only salvation. In the same way, God hates spinal cord injury, yet he permitted it for the sake of Christ in you—as well as in others."[3]

I remember meeting Joni when I was a child and thinking, *Wow, I really don't have any excuses for not following God*. The importance of knowing the stories of champions of the faith is vital for our surviving difficult circumstances. We need to hear that others have faced the unimaginable and accomplished the impossible through the power of God, who "will not fail you or forsake you" (Deut. 31:6). Thankfully, God promises to hold our hand and heart in the midst of suffering, confusion, and waiting.

We live our lives believing this world is about us, what we want, what our goals are, and who we are trying to be, but every once in a while, God steps in to slow us down and remind us that "we are but dust" (Ps. 103:14). Finding purpose in the seasons we never would have chosen for ourselves is imperative for surviving suffering.

Suffering tempts us to look inward and become consumed with ourselves. As we saw in chapter 3, renowned psychologist John Bradshaw explains that people with depression talk only about themselves for the same reason a person with a toothache talks only about his toothache—their pain is all they can think about, so it is all they can talk about.[4] During my forty-nine days of bedrest, having nurses constantly checking on me and spending hours a day hooked up to monitors, I was tempted to believe this time was about me. It would have been so easy to say, "You know, God, You really got me in a bad situation here. I'm sure You would understand if I just took some time off from my spiritual life and let You comfort me." Instead, I asked God every day to show me His purpose for my hospital stay.

We will never know God is all we need until God is all we have.

Nothing is an accident, and everything is an opportunity when we see things the way God sees them. When we care about what God cares about, we will not be bored or disappointed. There is always something to do to further God's kingdom, which takes care of any idle time or unwanted circumstance. We will never know God is all we need until God is all we have.

Growing Stronger through Suffering

In no way, shape, or form am I a "gamer," but I did play Super Mario Brothers in my younger years. There I would be, just trying to get Luigi to level two and not be eaten by the gigantic flowers with teeth, when all of a sudden he would slide down a golden pipe and into an alternate reality. This world looked like where he had just been but also different. Characters were more powerful. The setting was darker. The challenges were harder. But Luigi had the ability to be stronger and earn rewards that were greater in value. Then after Luigi had done the best he could do through my limited video game skill set, he would climb up a golden pipe back into normal reality, having earned thousands of extra points and gained special skills to help him in the game.

Suffering is similar to getting to go into the bonus round of a video game to get extra points. Obedience is our secret weapon in the face of suffering. Choosing to walk with God instead of counter to Him in the midst of suffering makes it possible for us to grow stronger, earn rewards, and gain skills that are priceless.

The Nearness of God in Suffering

We think about how often we suffer or how much we have been through like we're watching a highlight reel on a sports channel. The ability we have to recall how much we have been wronged can at times resemble a scene from *Rain Man*, where the autistic savant character Raymond Babbitt counts every card in the deck. We know each hardship we have suffered by heart. We have rehearsed the wrong done to us over and over. We have our suffering memorized and can recall each indignation at a moment's notice as soon as we see or experience anything resembling the same hurt. What about God? What must it do to His heart to see His children suffering at the hand of sin over and over, decade after decade, century after century? God comes especially near to us in times of suffering. I think perhaps watching His children suffer touches the heart of God in a way that draws His attention and magnifies His love.

Of course, God is powerful enough to stop anything and often does. The thought of what we have been spared from but have no awareness of is nothing short of haunting. How many times has God nudged us to go a different way home, avoiding a fatal car wreck? How many times has God woken us in the middle of the night, just in time to turn a light on and ward off an intruder about to break in? The possibilities are endless, and God's protection is certain. God promises the ultimate rectification of sin when Jesus comes back to redeem fallen creation and call His children home.

Joseph—An Example of Suffering with Faithfulness

Joseph had a thriving relationship with God in the midst of his suffering. Time and again the Bible includes the phrase, "But God was with Joseph," after nearly every trial Joseph faced.

Isn't God with every Christian? Yes, we all have his Holy Spirit; He loves all of us equally, He listens to our prayers, and His salvation is sufficient to cover the sin of everyone who believes in Jesus. But when we care about what God cares about, when we are trying to further His purpose, and when we are walking in obedience instead of disobedience, this opens the door to God being with us instead of having to discipline us.

Joseph did not cause his brothers to sell him into slavery. Joseph had no say over Potiphar's wife's false accusation. Joseph's big dream for his life probably was not to go to jail. However, Joseph chose to stay close and obedient to God in the middle of his trials in a way that resulted in God looking down from heaven and saying, "I'm going to be with him."

Hebrews 12:6 tells us, "Those whom the Lord loves He disciplines, and He scourges every son whom He receives." Obedience opens the door for God's blessing. Talking about good works and how they affect our relationship with God can be a slippery slope. We are not saved by good works but *for* good works. Ephesians 2:8–10 says, "For it is by grace you have been saved, through faith—and this is not from yourselves, it is the gift of God—not by works, so that no one can boast. For we are God's handiwork, created in Christ Jesus to do good works, which God prepared in advance for us to do" (NIV). With the power God gives us as Christians, we, like Joseph, can live in a way that causes God to walk with us.

Take Action

Obedience is a choice we have in the face of any challenge, trial, and temptation. Trials are God's vote of confidence in you. How can we obey in the midst of our suffering?

Remember What God Cares About

God cares more about changing you than He cares about changing your situation. This is a lesson Joseph had to learn through his intense time of trials and isolation. This is a lesson Jesus learned as He prayed in the Garden of Gethsemane for God to not make Him go to the cross, saying, "Father, if You are willing, remove this cup from Me; yet not My will, but Yours be done" (Luke 22:42).

Sometimes, no matter how hard we pray, God says no to our heartfelt requests. When we surrender and watch God show up and show off, we can see why He said no and be grateful He did.

Not long ago, a woman contacted me who was discouraged because she had prayed big things, she had rejoiced with those who rejoiced and wept with those who wept (Rom. 12:15), and she had trusted God to provide—but at the age of sixty-four, she knew her dreams of a biological child were destined to stay dreams. What hope is there when God appears not to listen to us? Did we not pray hard enough, not read our Bible long enough, or not seek enough wise counsel?

God has a plan that exceeds our understanding. As the saying goes, when we can't see His hand, we must trust His heart.

Ask God to Show You His Purpose for You

Witnessing is a way to make any day extraordinary. Forty-nine days of staying in the same hospital room, looking out the same window, and eating the same hospital food became very monotonous. Telling people about Jesus in the midst of wondering if my babies were going to live helped me remember the true purpose of life.

The day I was admitted to the hospital, I started asking God to show me His purpose for me in the hospital, with the staff, doctors, other patients, and my family. I had two nurses who were interested in Christianity. They would often ask me questions while they were checking on the babies.

One day I felt so pressed to present the gospel that I told God, "Okay, I will witness to them if You provide an open door." Right then, the nurse said, "I know this is weird, but I actually need to sit on your bed for the next twenty minutes to monitor the triplets." This gave me a wonderful opportunity to share the gospel with her. This happened with another nurse who needed to monitor one of the triplets, providing yet another opportunity for me to share God's plan of redemption.

Focusing on other people's relationship with God and honestly caring about their eternal destiny helped me to look past my present situation and purposefully pursue the spiritual needs of others, and it will do the same for you.

I did not always feel like caring about other people while in such a dire medical state. I am convinced that allowing God to use me as a messenger of the gospel is what got me through the long hours, days, and months. This is our secret weapon against the enemy. No matter what God allows to come into our lives, we have the opportunity to make it purposeful.

> *This is our secret weapon against the enemy. No matter what God allows to come into our lives, we have the opportunity to make it purposeful.*

Commit to Obedience in Suffering

Suffering provides us with two paths: the road of perseverance and the road of despair. These two paths are not destinies but decisions. You and I decide how we are going to respond in the face of adversity.

Because struggling with eating disorders is part of my testimony and the path that led me into the psychological field, I like working with people who are facing similar struggles. One of the first techniques I teach clients who struggle with eating disorders is to say out loud, "I'm choosing to do this," before engaging in their eating disorder behavior. I remember a young woman in her thirties who was furious that I asked her to say this out loud before she purged. She had struggled on and off with eating disorders since childhood and was adamant that she would not comply with the assignment. I asked her, "Why don't you want to say, 'I'm choosing to do this' when bingeing and purging?" She quickly answered, "Because if I say that, I no longer have an excuse."

This woman had every right to have developed a maladaptive coping skill. Given her horrific abuse history, I wouldn't have faulted her for any disorder or addiction she had developed as a way to cope with the trauma in her past. However, we must understand the difference between circumstances that are not our choice and the responses that are our choice. The suffering may be something in which we truly had no choice and no responsibility, no possibility of avoidance—something in which we truly are victims. This woman had no say in the years of childhood abuse she suffered. I will even go so far as to say that at the beginning stages of her eating disorder, she did not have much of a choice because of her intense need as a child to cope with the abuse.

However, there comes a point, usually as adults, when we have to separate the suffering from our response to the suffering. One of the great things about being an adult is having the ability to see the truth and change our response. Having a choice is not an insult; it's our secret weapon. God deeply cares about those suffering.

The Reward for Obedience

Staying obedient during times of suffering puts us in the best place to receive God's help, perspective, deliverance, and blessing. Disobedience in suffering is making the choice to suffer twice—first from suffering and then from the consequences of not following the One who has allowed the suffering. God richly rewards those who stay obedient in the wait, in the questions, in the darkness.

One of the greatest promises in the Bible for those with broken hearts and tearstained faces is found in Revelation 21:4. When Jesus comes back, and death and sorrow are no more, "He will wipe away every tear from their eyes; and there will no longer be any death; there will no longer be any mourning, or crying, or pain; the first things have passed away." Until that day comes, we have a choice to run to or run away from the One who has promised to see us through.

8

Unanswered Prayers

> God . . . can bring blessing from my problems and my
> pain and my unanswered prayer.
>
> Anne Graham Lotz

As a little girl, I always wondered how people were chosen to give their testimonies at the annual church Thanksgiving service. Did the ministers vote on who had the best story of the year? Did they decide in whose life God had worked in the most miraculous ways? Who could share the most heartwarming story, making the audience feel thankful for their toothbrush? While I'm still not certain of the process for selecting those testimonies, one thing is for certain: no one is ever asked to share a testimony of how God disappointed them. Stories of unanswered prayers are not what we want to hear. We want to hear the good stories. We want to hear the miraculous stories. We want to hear about the hope others found, because maybe that means there is hope for us.

I recently watched a live video on social media where around seventy-five people were praying and singing to God as a young mom was dying after giving birth to her daughter. I don't know how I ended up finding the video, but once I joined, I couldn't stop watching. I joined the thousands who were watching this powerful scene of believers crying out to God to protect the woman's life and spare her child from growing up without a mother. I was so overwhelmed with emotion that I began interceding in prayer for the new mom as well. I remember thinking, *There is no way God will let her die. Look at all of us praying for her. He has to let her live. I know He will.* I called Ryan to come in from the other room, and he began praying too. Before we knew it, as we looked up at the video, someone announced that the new mother had just passed away. The Christians gathered in the hospital room kept singing and praising God. I said, "What?" I was mad. I was hurt. I was disappointed in God for letting her die. Then the camera zoomed in on a young man who appeared to be the woman's husband, and my feelings and thoughts were readjusted as I saw this heartbroken man still singing praises to God.

When God says no, it provides unique opportunities for us to say yes to trusting Him like never before.

How can we have faith that surpasses the pains of this world? How can we keep singing and praising God when He doesn't answer how we want Him to answer, how we prayed for Him to answer, or how we trusted Him to answer? In his book *A Grief Observed*, C. S. Lewis describes the grief he experienced after losing his wife. He says, "God had not been trying an experiment on my faith or love in order to find out their quality. He already knew it. It was I who didn't."[1] When God says no, it provides unique opportunities for us to say yes to trusting Him like never before.

In his country hit "Unanswered Prayers," Garth Brooks famously sang about the joy he felt when he looked back on God not answering his prayer requests, because there was something much better in his future than he could have imagined back then.

How do we thank God for unanswered prayers? How do we continue to follow God in the midst of them? Life is too short to spend it heartbroken, discouraged, or chasing dreams that are never meant to be. We ask God to help us let go of the desires that are not from Him and hold on with all ferocity to the ones that are.

We ask God to help us let go of the desires that are not from Him and hold on with all ferocity to the ones that are.

There is a closeness about letting God hold us during times of uncertainty that we don't usually experience when daily life is running smoothly. Times of waiting are times of opportunity. As I mentioned earlier, my dad likes to say, "Waiting time does not have to be wasted time." Though our situation may surprise us, there is incredible reassurance knowing that nothing surprises God.

"All Things Happen for a Reason"?

For as long as I can remember, I have loved quotes. Whether from authors, celebrities, biblical characters, presidents, or anyone clever enough to end up on a bumper sticker, I love reading quotes. I'm probably the person Hallmark has in mind when they make their greeting cards.

One day, at my local gas station in downtown Dallas, I walked over to the greeting card section while waiting to get my car washed. As I read through the quotes on the cards, I saw one that read, "Everything happens for a reason—American Proverb." I almost laughed out loud, until I became saddened by the realization of the untold numbers of people who firmly believe this phrase, not knowing it is a paraphrase of a Bible verse and an incomplete one at that.

"All things happen for a reason" may be comforting when we lose our job or break up with someone, believing that when one door closes another opens. But this saying is not very comforting when we get a bad doctor's report or lose a loved one to desertion or death.

I remember counseling a young woman who had intense guilt over believing she had made the wrong medical decision and had caused her mother's death. She was overwhelmed and felt abandoned by the God she believed she could trust. Another patient in the counseling group said to her, "I know you are sad, but remember all things happen for a reason." In the blink of an eye, this woman's disposition completely changed from incredible sadness to intense anger. The ultimate cause of her mother's death was of no comfort to her. What was missing? Why did this sentiment not comfort this grieving daughter?

Because "all things happen for a reason" misses the point, purpose, and second half of the verse. In full, Romans 8:28–29 reads,

> We know that God causes all things to work together for good to those who love God, to those who are called according to

His purpose. For those whom He foreknew, He also predestined to become conformed to the image of His Son, so that He would be the firstborn among many brethren.

All things work together for the good of those who love God, yes, absolutely. But the "good" promised is not necessarily what we've written on our carefully formulated life plan. The "good" this passage refers to is to "become conformed to the image of His Son." Whatever comes into our lives has the opportunity and purpose to make us more like Christ. Whether or not we let that happen is our choice.

"Week 34, December 30"

The day we found out we were having triplets, I was ecstatic. I had never been more thrilled, excited, or overcome with joy in my life. But that night I couldn't sleep, as I had also never been so overcome with anxiety. I spent the next seven months Googling possible complications. I think at times I was even trying to out-Google God! I would get to a certain week in my pregnancy, read about some potential complication that I had gotten past, and, if I'm being totally honest, think, *Okay, great. Now even God can't let such-and-such happen.* I spent a lot of time believing that God and I were on different sides. This only brings fear, because if God is not on your side, then you're all alone, and all alone is a scary place to be.

Triplet pregnancies are always considered high-risk. I thought my pregnancy would be high-risk only if a certain issue developed or if something went wrong. But no; from the get-go, me and the three other people I now represented were considered high-risk. I constantly quizzed my doctors about when I would be in the clear to give birth to healthy babies. The doctors told me that at twenty-four weeks the babies would be considered viable; at twenty-five weeks they would reach a milestone of 90 percent chance of survival, but if we could get to week thirty-four, that would really put us in the clear.[2] I would think, *At week thirty-four, even God can't keep them from surviving.*

Again, I was caught in the thought that God and I were on different sides. This prayer request went out to anyone and everyone: "Pray for Julia and the triplets to make it to Week 34, December 30." "Week 34, December 30" was like a mantra that we recited, meditated upon, and brought before the Lord countless times a day. "Week 34, December 30" was the prayer request given to every prayer board, every staff meeting, every deacons' meeting, all the prayer partners of our church, and in all of our social media posts. "Please, God, please let us make it that far."

During my forty-nine days of bedrest, I would beg God from my hospital bed: "Please, God, let us make it to week thirty-four." Every week, the doctor would come into my room trying to encourage me with another week met. I was not satisfied. It wasn't week thirty-four, so it was not good enough. I would even tell non-Christians I met at the hospital about praying for week thirty-four.

I tried everything I could think of to push God's hand toward doing what I wanted. I constantly fought between thinking I had a lot of control to being in near despair at the truth that I had none. Bedrest was the loneliest experience of my life. Day after day, night after night, when visiting hours were over and I was all alone, when Ryan had gone to work, and when my mom had gone home, I was left to my own thoughts and fears.

The nurses were constantly preparing for when I would "break." When would I stop being so joyful? When would I give in to the panic and fear? That moment came on day forty-eight.

On that day, everything changed. I looked around at my four walls that had gone from being decorated with flowers to Thanksgiving decor and then to Christmas lights. I looked out the same window that I had spent close to 576 hours looking out of. My peace, joy, and endurance were gone, and I had to get out of there.

I called my doctor, Ryan, and my friend Parris, and I pleaded with them to let me leave. I felt as if all my emotions had been pushed back like the ocean in a tsunami and were now rushing in, threatening to overtake me. I couldn't do it anymore. I wouldn't do it anymore. Something had to change, now!

The doctor told me it was too late in my high-risk pregnancy to be discharged. The news was crippling, and all I could do was pray. With tears streaming down my face, I cried out to God, "I cannot do this anymore! I know You will help me, and I'll do whatever You ask of me. But if there is any way, I need my babies to come as soon as they can come and be healthy. Holy Spirit, I am so distraught and confused. I need You to pray on my behalf." Then I fell asleep almost immediately.

I woke up feeling so rested and so peaceful that I even put makeup on, did my hair, and ate breakfast before my one of two weekly outings: sonogram day. An hour later, the doctor informed us that today was going to be delivery day. We were told not to expect to hear the babies crying or screaming. There would be twenty-four people in the delivery room—a separate NICU team for each baby. Blair was born at 2.12 lbs. Barrett was born at 3.5 lbs. Blake was born at 3.1 lbs. All screaming, all crying, all surviving sixty-four days in the NICU. All home the night before our nine-year wedding anniversary.

To this day, I can remember the date we prayed for, December 30, better than the triplets' actual birthday. I have never been as thankful for unanswered prayers as I was on December 6, 2017, when we met our babies weeks before the day we had prayed for but also right on time.

God is not limited by our imagination. We cannot put Him in a box and tell Him how to act or answer. This doesn't mean we don't do anything or ask everything; this means we consider what God tells us in Isaiah 55:8–9: "'My thoughts are not your thoughts, nor are your ways My ways,' declares the LORD. 'For as the heavens are higher than the earth, so are My ways higher than your ways and My thoughts than your thoughts.'"

Joseph—An Example of Persevering through Unanswered Prayers

How many times must Joseph have asked God to change his circumstances? When he realized his brothers hated him? When he realized he was about to be sold into slavery? When he was thrown into prison? When he was forgotten by the chief baker and taster? I'm going to have to say yes to all, not because there is biblical text saying so but because Joseph was human. Yet, time and again, we see him persevere in faith in spite of undoubtedly experiencing what he perceived as unanswered prayers.

How was Joseph able to stay committed to God in the midst of so much uncertainty? He gives us the summation of all he learned through his time of suffering and waiting in what is one of the most well-known verses in the Bible. Like a movie perfectly plotted, with a heartwarming cinematic moment demanding a standing ovation from the audience, Joseph was finally reunited with his brothers. Looking back on all the events that had brought them to that moment, Joseph said, "As for you, you meant evil against me, but God meant it for good in order to bring about this present result, to preserve many people alive" (Gen. 50:20).

There was nothing good about Joseph suffering at the hands of his brothers. However, God was able to use this evil act to move Joseph to become second in command of Egypt. Similarly, there was nothing good about Jesus being tortured and murdered on the cross. But that was the perspective of Friday. On Sunday, when Jesus rose from the dead, He made it possible for anyone who accepted His free gift of salvation to go to heaven. God used Jesus's suffering to accomplish our salvation.

Nothing comes into our lives that God has not allowed and has not deemed for a specific purpose.

God hates evil, but He is also powerful enough to use whatever happens in our lives for our good and His glory. Nothing comes into our lives that God has not allowed and has not deemed for a specific purpose.

Take Action

How can we take hope during seasons when God is not answering our prayers—or not answering them in the way we hoped He would?

Remember Your Purpose

There is a specific purpose for your life that is not dependent on anything other than you following Christ. Nothing that happens or doesn't happen changes the plan God has for you. God's Word never speaks of multiple wills for us but only one will: God's. I remember talking to a wise woman in our church about how I sometimes wondered what would have happened if I had made other decisions. If I had chosen to stay at Baylor instead of going to Dallas Baptist University. If I had chosen to pursue being a news anchor instead of a licensed professional counselor.

She spoke one of the most comforting truths to me: "Julia, there are not several plans for your life. There is not an alternate reality where you make other choices and your life turns out another way. There is one plan, and you are living it." No purpose that God has for you can be changed or compromised by us or anyone else. We are not powerful enough to mess up God's plan.

Don't Turn Away from God When You Need Him the Most

A main part of Ryan's job is spiritually preparing high school students for college. "Every year is our senior year," Ryan and I often joke with each other as we hurriedly write recommendation letters for scholarship applications on be-

half of students who are just a little too close for comfort
to their deadlines. We attend, plan, and speak at the gradu-
ations, baccalaureates, senior parties, senior recognitions,
senior Sundays, and senior trips.

Every year we watch students we have poured our lives
into take one of two roads. They either follow Christ in
college or they decide to take a break from their faith. Ryan
says to them, every chance he gets, "Don't turn away from
God when you need Him the most." College is often when
people decide what occupation they will pursue, where they
will live, with whom they will be friends, what direction they
want their life to go, and with whom they will spend the rest
of their life. These decisions need God's direction.

The same crossroad opportunity is true for us in times of
waiting. We have one of two roads to choose. We can turn
our backs on God, deciding He doesn't really care since He
isn't answering how we think He should, or we can choose
daily, sometimes hourly, to come to Him with our hurt, fears,
and questions. Waiting is lonely enough without spending
it apart from the only One who knows the reason for the
waiting. Waiting times are opportunities to truly get to know
the heart of the One who calls you His.

Cling to What Is Truly Good

The best way to combat anxiety, lies, depression, confusion,
social media comparison, and most other problems in the
world is to practice telling ourselves the truth. I remember saying this in a counseling group one time, and a man unashamedly asked, "What exactly is truth?" Truth is what God says
about us or about our situation. In times of waiting, suffering,
praying, dreaming, and hoping, we must cling to what is true.

The Bible tells us in Philippians 4:8 to meditate, think on, and dwell on "whatever is true." This doesn't mean we just walk around all day saying what we want to be true. We don't stand at the kitchen sink washing dishes continually saying to ourselves, "One day I'm going to be able to hire a staff of ten people to take care of my house, and I'll never lift a finger to do another chore again!" It's a nice dream but probably not realistic. It means we constantly tell ourselves God's truth about us and our situation. God says we are worthy. God says nothing is impossible with Him. God says He will never leave us.

> *Everything that is allowed into our lives has the purpose of making us more like Christ.*

Though God is working out all things for our good and His glory, remember what is "truly good" is God making us into the image of Christ. That is His goal for us. Everything that is allowed into our lives has the purpose of making us more like Christ.

Remember We Don't Know the Full Story

While our full story has been written, our full story has yet to be revealed. One rainy day on the way home from her mother's funeral, a little girl asked her dad how long she was going to be sad. How long would she cry? How long would she be heartbroken? Her father held back his own tears and tried to find a way to explain grief and loss to his little girl.

When the funeral limousine drove inside a tunnel on the highway, he realized he had a good analogy to share about grief. "Sweetheart," he explained, "grief is like a tunnel we must pass through to get to the other side."

On this side of eternity, we will not know the full story of why God has allowed something painful to come into our lives. When you are going through a struggle and feel like you are in a dark tunnel, remember there is light on the other side. We cannot rush the process of grief. It takes time to go through the process of grieving and healing. It takes time for our emotions to heal as well. But the good news is that God has wonderful things waiting for us on the other side! As Psalm 30:5 reminds us, "Weeping may last for the night, but a shout of joy comes in the morning."

Thank God for All Things

In her book *The Hiding Place*, Holocaust survivor Corrie ten Boom tells the story of how God taught her to be thankful for all things. Corrie and her sister, Betsie, were held in the Nazi concentration camp Ravensbruck, which was filthy, overcrowded, and infested by fleas.

They had been able to smuggle a New Testament into the camp, and they read, "Rejoice always; pray without ceasing; in everything give thanks; for this is God's will for you in Christ Jesus" (1 Thess. 5:16–18).

Betsie began applying the command "in everything give thanks." She thanked God for assigning her to the same barracks as Corrie. She thanked God for the faulty inspection that had enabled them to smuggle in the Bible. She thanked God for the suffocating crowds, which meant more people could hear the gospel. She even thanked God for the fleas.

That was too much for Corrie, who was horrified by the fleas. But Betsy insisted, so Corrie gave in and prayed, thanking God even for the fleas.

Over the next several months, a wonderful, but curious, thing happened. They found that the guards never entered their barracks.

This meant that the young women were not assaulted.

It also meant that they were able to do the unthinkable, which was to hold open Bible studies and prayer meetings in the heart of a Nazi concentration camp.

Through this, countless numbers of women came to faith in Christ.

Only at the end did they discover why the guards had left them alone and would not enter into their barracks.

It was because of the fleas.[3]

God has a purpose for our waiting time, for our unanswered prayers, for the seasons of life that seem to threaten our faith and future. Let us let go of the dreams that are not from God and hold on with all ferocity to the ones that are from Him.

9

Dream Big, Give Thanks, and Have Fun

In between goals there is this thing called life that must be lived and enjoyed.

Sid Caesar

Who can forget their first Disney movie? I was four years old when my dad took me to see *The Jungle Book* at a locally owned theater in a West Texas town. It was the best day of my life to date. There is a certain magic and genius in Disney movies, productions, and theme parks that has the ability to transcend children and adults alike into a happier state. Perhaps the main reason Disney has become a multibillion-dollar empire is because its founder realized something that few other people have: adults need to have as much fun as children.

Walt Disney's philosophy of fun may have been questionable to skeptics watching from the sidelines as he built his empire. However, the Disney dream has continued to grow even four decades after Walt's death. The Disney Company is now the world's largest independent media conglomerate, with worldwide influence in movies, publishing, music, television, and merchandising, plus cruise ships and fourteen theme parks around the world.

Having fun is a prescription that fit into Walt Disney's take on life, but more importantly celebrating, rejoicing, and being grateful are found in the Bible. These directives can change your day, your year, and your life. They are both timeless and scriptural.

A "Messy" Ministry

The triplets were nearly impossible to feed when they came home from the hospital. Barrett took a combination of breastmilk and added calories with one kind of reflux medication. Blair took formula with added calories and a different brand of reflux medication that must be manually mixed and allowed to sit before giving. Blake took a different brand of formula with a different amount of added calories and no reflux medication. If the wrong baby was given the wrong milk product, the result could be fatal, because breastmilk was too thin for two of the triplets due to their prematurity and had caused bradycardias (slowing of the heart) in the NICU. Then, after feeding, all three had to sit up for forty-five minutes and be closely watched because of their terrible reflux. Oh, and a burp cloth and syringe had to be kept close by, because they easily choked on their spit-up. Just in case this doesn't seem like a lot to keep up with, the regimen kept three professional nannies who had spent decades in childcare from accepting our nanny position.

I felt guilty for finding it so difficult to feed these babies whom I had begged God to allow me to bring home. I had prayed continually before they were born, and now I was barely able to smile out of exhaustion. People told me this was normal, but I wasn't okay with it being my normal. Something had to change. I needed to reclaim my sense of joy and gratitude.

I decided to start posting videos of Ryan and me dancing and singing with the babies on social media, mainly so I would always have a record of this time. One Sunday, an elderly woman came up to me at church in tears and said, "Thank you for posting your dancing videos with the triplets with all the laundry in the background."

I replied, "Oh, thanks. I'm glad my messy house encouraged you."

She then grabbed my hand with tears in her eyes and said, "No, you don't get it. My mom would not ever let a single thing in our house be out of place. It was miserable." All I could do was tell her I was sorry, as she walked away.

What that encounter taught me was that having fun despite the "mess" of daily life can be a ministry to others. The motto for our student ministry is "keep it spiritual and keep it fun." Being spiritual and having fun do not have to be mutually exclusive. Enjoying our lives is a way of saying "thank you" to God for the good things in our lives

Having fun despite the "mess" of daily life can be a ministry to others.

and reminds those watching of God's giving and gracious character.

Maybe the goal of having fun seems just a tad shallow to you. But according to neuroscientists, having fun is essential to optimal brain function! God has wired our brains to function better when having fun.

Whenever we are engaged in a task or subject, our neurons release dopamine, a chemical that helps our brains transmit signals. Dopamine affects the processes in our brains that control our emotions and ability to experience pleasure. The more interested we are in a particular subject or activity, the more dopamine is released and the better we are able to remember it.[1]

When things seem out of order, when your life is getting too far away from how you know it is supposed to be, it's time to rally the troops and get a new battle cry. Laughter is timeless, and joy is invincible. That's why the Bible says, "Taste and see that the LORD is good" (Ps. 34:8). The Lord is always good; we just have to take time to slow down and notice the good things He has done for us!

Why We Need to Celebrate

The year we experienced so many lost pregnancies, Ryan and I were being continually disappointed in our own lives. When God seemed to be blessing everyone else around us, dreaming big, giving thanks, and having fun ensured our survival as a couple and kept our faith in God strong. Now, with our triplets at home, celebrating allowed us to stay focused on the present and enjoy what God had for us in that moment. But after nearly a year of not being able to do much other than worry about the health of three babies, I had a lot of catching up to do that was weighing on my mind. I had two book manuscripts due, a full-time job, was filming a TV show, and was remodeling a house—in the midst of parenting seven-month-old triplets. Then I read this wise quote attributed to writer and actor Sid Caesar: "In between goals there is this thing called life that must be lived and enjoyed." In the middle of my goals, I had to slow down and celebrate the special moments I would never get back with my only children.

I just read about a family who spent all summer driving across the country in a motor coach with their five children in order to be able to let go and live in the moment. They said they struggled so much with control that they decided it was necessary to leave it all behind and head west with no plan or schedule. Living in the moment is not something often preached from the pulpit, but it is a message many of us need to hear.

The saying "Satan will either make you sin or make you busy" rings true for too many of us. Working hard is not wrong. But working so hard and so long that we forget why we are working and who we are doing it for is not good. Because of my propensity to work with the laser focus of a bunny with a carrot tied to a stick in front of her, I have grown up with my dad saying, "Julia, don't wish your life away." That phrase always helps me stop and smell the roses.

At a recent church event, I sat next to a woman who was the most joyful person I had ever met. I had so much fun talking to her that I honestly did not want the dinner to be over because of how refreshing I found her. She was the definition of "My yoke is easy and My burden is light" (Matt. 11:30).

She had also lost all four of her children and her husband and didn't have any family anywhere close to her, yet she spent her life being involved in her church and devoted to her friends, and telling anyone who would listen how great her God is. How could she be so joyful after experiencing so much loss? It is possible to enjoy life when you know the Author of life. When I grow up, I want to be just like her.

It is possible to enjoy life when you know the Author of life.

Celebrating makes life worth living. I hate to put this idea out there, but I also kind of have to say it: What if the thing you're waiting on doesn't happen, and you waste significant time in your life being unhappy and unfulfilled? I love this quote from the movie *Ever After*: "And while Cinderella and her prince did live happily ever after, the point is, gentlemen, that they lived."[2]

Dreaming is good. Working is godly. But while working to get to the mountaintop of whatever we have decided is our ultimate goal, we must be able to live in the valley of waiting. We must celebrate right where we are.

What Happens When We Don't Celebrate

"Hi! I'm Ruby!" a jovial teenage girl announced as she plopped down in the Sunday school class I teach. The rest of the class turned to observe her upon her arrival. She was the most full-of-life, joyful, and friendly person I had ever met. Her smile seemed to be stuck permanently on her face, and her eyes sparkled. As she introduced herself, the class found out that she was visiting our church with a family member, but she was not a Christian. As I looked around the room and even gave my own morning behavior a quick examination, I thought how much more joyful this girl who didn't know the Lord seemed than we did. Is joy a given for Christians? Is happiness a choice?

Is some of the distinction more of a personality difference, or is it really all spiritual? If joy is the right of Christians, then what is missing in so many of our lives? Why are some people who don't know the Lord happier, friendlier, and more joyful than many of those who do? We can theorize all day, but one thing is for sure: misery is not the destiny of a child of God.

Being a Christian means there is always something to celebrate, because every day we live in the freedom and peace that we belong to the One who has defeated death.

> *Misery is not the destiny of a child of God.*

We are able to hold our heads up and claim in our hearts, minds, and relationships, "If God is for us, who is against us?" (Rom. 8:31).

So why do so many of us live our lives defeated and unhappy? We have forgotten how to celebrate. Proverbs 17:22 tells us, "A joyful heart is good medicine, but a broken spirit dries up the bones." When we are merry, we laugh, we are joyful, we are full of life, and we are cheerful. When we are merry, we radiate the goodness of God and the hope of the gospel that is available to others.

A miserable Christian is a walking billboard for why not to follow Jesus. There are, of course, appropriate times for grief and sadness. Ecclesiastes 3:4 says there is "a time to weep and . . . a time to mourn." We are following the example of Christ when we weep for the loved ones we lose. Jesus wept for his beloved friend Lazarus (John 11:35), and we will feel intense loss this side of heaven for those taken away from us. Pain is the price of love.

However, sadness is not the same as misery. Christopher Reeve is attributed as saying, after being paralyzed from the neck down, "Pain is inevitable; misery is a choice."[3] This profound truth came from a man who called himself an atheist most of his life. Misery is a state not meant for one who knows the resurrected Christ. Let me take a minute here and say that I'm not interested in "faking it until you make it." We should not ask more of ourselves than God does. He is not disappointed when we have emotions. Expressing our emotions actually allows us to connect with God. I want us all to find a newfound love for daily putting on the armor of God, described in Ephesians 6:10–18, which was created for us to be able to withstand anything meant to rob us of the joy we have in knowing God is for us, not against us. True transformation in the way we experience life is possible when we are able to see our life through God's eyes.

> *True transformation in the way we experience life is possible when we are able to see our life through God's eyes.*

As I mentioned earlier, the year we were trying to get pregnant and experienced three miscarriages, thirteen of our friends announced their pregnancies. It was rough, to say the least. After every heartache I would inevitably end up seeing another pregnancy announcement, be invited to another baby shower, or hear another woman at work being congratulated on her pregnancy—whereupon I would shut the door to my office and cry.

I honestly did not know how I was going to survive until God gave me Romans 12:15 as a theme verse: "Rejoice with those who rejoice, and weep with those who weep." Ryan and I made the choice to celebrate God's work in others' lives in the midst of processing our own losses. This choice was the armor that saved us from the dark road of bitterness. Praying big things during this season in our lives meant praying for others, for their pregnancies, for their marriages, and for their babies.

The choice to join others in celebrating God's work, even when it doesn't directly impact us, can be our key to unlock joy in times of trials.

A God Who Celebrates

The parable of the lost son in Luke 15 is my favorite example of celebration in the Bible because it is an example of God celebrating. Putting ourselves in the place of the prodigal son is easy for anyone who has lived on earth for more than a day. Reading this story of a son leaving his dad only to find out how much he needed him, we feel the shame, the anger, the urge to run and rebel, and the relief when we are welcomed back by loved ones, especially by the One who loved us first. There are many applications for this heartwarming parable that Jesus tells in order to explain how God responds when sinners turn to Him. God loves the far off. God loves the messed up. God loves the seemingly unredeemable.

When the father saw his prodigal son returning home, he said, "'Quickly bring out the best robe and put it on him, and put a ring on his hand and sandals on his feet; and bring the fattened calf, kill it, and let us eat and celebrate; for this son of mine was dead and has come to life again; he was lost and has been found.' And they began to celebrate" (Luke 15:22–24). God loves to celebrate when we return to Him.

Celebrating reminds us what is really important: other people and spreading the message of Jesus Christ. In a world intent on telling us that life is all about us, our social media followers, our weekend plans, our wardrobe, and our bank account, the parable of the prodigal son reminds us that life is about bringing people to Jesus.

As Christians, we have the most fulfilling calling possible: to bring people to heaven by telling them about salvation found in Jesus Christ. This calling depends on nothing except our willingness to accept the call. Picture Tom Cruise receiving his assignment in the *Mission Impossible* movies: "Your mission, should you choose to accept it . . ." will be the greatest adventure of your life, and your efforts will echo in eternity.

> *Celebrating reminds us what is really important: other people and spreading the message of Jesus Christ.*

Celebrating others allows us to become genuinely interested in God's work in other people's lives. It reminds us that we are all on the same team and have the same goal. And celebrating others reassures us that no personal circumstance can take away our collective purpose as soldiers in Christ's army.

"Rejoice Always"

Celebrating can also be a secret weapon against defeat, discouragement, and disinterest. The first two words in that list probably didn't surprise you, but what do I mean by *disinterest*? A lot of our unhappiness is because we are focused inward instead of outward.

As I mentioned earlier, individuals who struggle with depression are some of the most self-centered people you will ever meet. I don't say this insensitively but as a licensed professional counselor who has treated hundreds of depressed individuals because of my passion for helping people live the lives God created for them. There is a chicken-and-egg relationship with depression and self-centeredness, but the fact remains that there is a correlation. One of the first suggestions for someone struggling with depression is for them to find ways to help other people. Helping others creates a necessary shift in focus, allowing depressed individuals the opportunity to think about something other than the pain they are feeling.

I have a sign in my kitchen that says, "'Rejoice Always.' 1 Thessalonians 5:16." It is in my kitchen because every time I am annoyed by the dishes, the mundane household tasks, and the triplets' feeding schedule on a continuous loop, I am reminded that I always have a choice. "Rejoice always" reminds me there is always something I can be thankful for, and there is always a way God is working around me that I can rejoice in. I have a choice to be joyful. I have a choice regardless of what the day brings.

Satan can't devour someone who doesn't let him in.

I am convinced that what many people call "bad days" are really just bad thinking patterns. The fact that we have control over our thoughts is our secret weapon against an enemy who "prowls around like a roaring lion, seeking someone to devour" (1 Pet. 5:8). Satan can't devour someone who doesn't let him in.

Joseph—An Example of Celebration

Joseph dreamed big, gave thanks to God for sustaining him in unspeakable suffering, and celebrated with his brothers when they were reunited. When he saw his brothers after years of separation, Genesis 45:1–2 tells us, "Joseph could not control himself before all those who stood by him, and he cried, 'Have everyone go out from me.' So there was no man with him when Joseph made himself known to his brothers. He wept so loudly that the Egyptians heard it, and the household of Pharaoh heard of it."

Weeping so loudly an entire palace heard about the emotional outburst may not seem like the best verse to prove Joseph celebrated. However, it is important to see Joseph's humanity. He was distraught. He was hurt. He had been abandoned, mistreated, and left for dead by his brothers. How many times must he have dreamed of this moment of reunion? How many years passed before Joseph was able to be in this place of wanting reconciliation, of wanting to see his brothers again face-to-face? I wonder if his visualization of this moment had moved from a well-crafted argument of ringing them up one side and down the other, to deciding he never wanted to see them again, to a place of realizing no matter what had happened, he missed them and desired reconciliation more than anything.

Joseph had an incredible, emotional outpouring of hurt, anger, sadness, loneliness, and joy that must have struck his brothers to their core. Joseph, the second in command of

Egypt, was in an instant brought back to being that young man sold into slavery, weeping, crying, and mourning in the presence of his abusers. Then Joseph eloquently articulated a perspective on suffering that is nothing short of extraordinary—a perspective that can only be seen by someone looking at God and not at their circumstances.

Joseph encouraged his brothers by saying to them,

> Do not be grieved or angry with yourselves, because you sold me here, for God sent me before you to preserve life. . . . God sent me before you to preserve for you a remnant in the earth, and to keep you alive by a great deliverance. Now, therefore, it was not you who sent me here, but God; and He has made me a father to Pharaoh and lord of all his household and ruler over all the land of Egypt. (vv. 5, 7–8)

Wow. What a testament to how God can change our perspective on any circumstance! It is possible for all of us to see our situation through heavenly eyes when we are looking and listening for His purpose to be revealed.

Do not miss that Joseph's spiritual perspective came after he went through the very human process of grieving. God never asks us to be fake. God is not disappointed when we let our humanity show, as if emotions were something not from Him. God knows there is only so much we can take, and He promises that there is always more to our story—more He is doing, more He is accomplishing—more than anything we can imagine.

It is possible for all of us to see our situation through heavenly eyes when we are looking and listening for His purpose to be revealed.

Reunion is cause for celebration. Restoration is certainly cause for celebration. Knowing God is writing a bigger story that withstands anything this world throws at us is also cause for celebration.

Take Action

How can we learn to celebrate God's work in our lives and others' lives, even when we don't feel like it?

Don't Wish Your Life Away

If the challenge "Don't wish your life away" seems like a directive needed exclusively for those with a type A personality, then consider how many people are dissatisfied with where they are in life, their marriage status, their job, their income, or their relationship with God.

According to a recent study by the Gallup organization and the health care information service Sharecare, the "subjective well-being" of Americans is down across the nation. This detailed study surveyed more than 2.5 million people, examining how they felt in their everyday lives across key dimensions of well-being, including physical health, personal and family relationships, financial and economic security, a sense of purpose, and connection to one's community. The overall results? "From 2016 to 2017, America saw its largest year-over-year drop in well-being in the 10 years that Gallup has tracked these data. Furthermore, 21 states registered absolute declines in their levels of well-being, and not a single state showed a statistically significant improvement in 2017."[4] The facts are clear: people today are increasingly dissatisfied with their lives.

If the majority of people in America—73 percent—report that they go online on a daily basis, and if 21 percent of Americans admit they go online "almost constantly,"[5] then most of America has a morning routine of comparing ourselves to others. I am now convinced that Satan is using social media to distract us from the real world, real relationships, and real callings God has for us.

> *Gratitude is the easiest way to stay in the moment.*

Gratitude is the easiest way to stay in the moment. Stop right now and thank God for at least five things in your life. I'm listening to my son Barrett make baby noises in the other room while I'm fervently trying to finish this manuscript, and isn't that what I could have only dreamed for a year ago?

Take Time to Rest

We either choose to rest, or God makes sure we do so. I learned to rest the hard way by being on medically ordered bedrest for forty-nine days. Rest is not an option but a command. God made us, which means He knows how our bodies and relationships will work best. And the One who knows us best says we need to relax at least one day a week. Resting is hard for some and easy for others. Resting allows our brain to settle, our emotions to calm, and our heart to have time to remember the purpose of this wonderful life: Jesus. Not us, not our to-do list, not our schedule, not our ten-year plan.

Many have dismissed the biblical commands to rest and meditate as only for Eastern religions. But these practices originated in the Bible and we are to be as devoted to them as we are to reading our Bible. Psalm 46:10 tells us, "Be still, and know that I am God; I will be exalted among the nations, I will be exalted in the earth" (NIV).

How can we be still in a world determined to keep our every second scheduled? I suggest that you pray first thing in the morning. Before you get out of bed, connect with Jesus. Hear from God before you hear from anyone else. Read Scripture before you interact or talk to anyone. Schedule your relaxation time and protect it.

Most of my stress comes from deadlines or projects that have no real stopping place until they are officially done. This makes it hard to relax. For me, I form my goal, I make a plan to accomplish that goal, I give myself grace, I work hard—and I schedule my worry time. I'm allowed to worry about these projects when I'm working on them, but after that time of the day is over, I don't talk about the project anymore and I don't worry about it anymore.

We have great control over what we think about and worry about—and whether we run ourselves ragged or spend time connecting with Jesus. We make time for the things that are important to us.

Give Thanks

Thankfulness changes everything. I was not immediately thankful every time my heart broke with another lost pregnancy. I had to search for thankfulness after each miscarriage. I had to pursue it. As the old axiom goes, I had to "act my way into a feeling, not feel my way into an action." I chose to thank God for everything I could think of in my life and in others' lives,

Thankfulness changes everything.

and it completely changed my demeanor and helped me bear what I thought was unbearable.

Have Fun

Walt Disney once reportedly said, "Laughter is America's most important export." Find ways to have fun. Ryan and I love developing our own holidays. So far we have "Celebrary," the month of February, which has our anniversary, Valentine's Day, and my birthday in a two-week period, and "Triprise," the annual celebration of when we found out God had answered our prayers for triplets. This year, we celebrated Triprise by taking our six-month-old triplets to the top of Reunion Tower in Dallas, told them their story, prayed and thanked God for answered prayer, and talked about what big prayers we wanted to pray for us and for them in the next year. Eventually we will help the triplets come up with their own big prayers and big dreams to share!

The Ultimate Good for Our Lives

Ecclesiastes 3:11 says, "He has made everything appropriate [with a purpose] in its time. He has also set eternity in their heart, yet so that man will not find out the work which God has done from the beginning even to the end." Remember that while we are dreaming big dreams and praying big things, the ultimate good that God has for our lives is making us like Christ. Celebrating others is loving them. Loving others is being Jesus to the world.

10

Never Give Up

Never give in, never give in, never, never, never, never—
in nothing, great or small, large or petty—never give in.

Winston Churchill

The ice-cold chill of the winter night stinging my face felt like the reality hitting me of what our lives had now become. It was month five of living in the hospital. Where had the year gone? I had spent the first two months on bedrest, praying, begging, and pleading with God to let our babies make it safely into the world. Then for the next three months, after they were born, we watched them fight for their lives as, I'm convinced, thousands fought for them in prayer.

I felt as if I was living in some weird alternate universe, a time warp where the outside world was a distant memory and my new reality was listening to my babies' heart rates fail, watching nurses rush in to resuscitate them, and praying with Ryan every night that we would wake up to still having three living premature babies. The NICU changes you. Seeing two- and three-pound newborns struggle to breathe is haunting. What a humbling picture of James 4:15: "If the Lord wills, we will live . . ."

Blair and Blake were still in the NICU at the hospital they had been born in, but Barrett had been admitted to another hospital just twenty-four hours after coming home. How was I going to muster the strength to start visiting my babies in two hospitals when I barely could muster the emotional, spiritual, and physical strength to make it to one? I was occasionally asked by hospital staff if I was okay, but how could I be okay when I didn't know what tomorrow or even the next hour would bring?

I had to rely heavily on a lesson God had taught me when I was twelve weeks' pregnant. At the time, I had made it through my first trimester and thought I was in the clear with the triplet pregnancy. If I'm being completely honest, I thought I had gotten to a place where even God couldn't take the triplets away. Not that He would do so arbitrarily. He is a good God. But with losing so many babies, the sinful thought in my mind was that I could get to a place physically where even God Himself could not end the pregnancy.

As I mentioned earlier, I was feeling confident about making it to the second trimester until I decided to Google "triplet moms." But when I sat down and opened up my computer to educate myself about moms of multiples, the first headline read something along the lines of, "New Mom of Triplets Dies a Few Days after Giving Birth." *What?* I felt as though I had the wind knocked out of me. I could not believe God would let something like that happen. *Doesn't He know how*

170

difficult triplet pregnancies are? Doesn't He understand how much those babies need their mom? I read a few more stories. The next was of a triplet mom who had lost her babies at twenty-two weeks, and another story was about a mother giving birth to stillborn triplets. I was horrified. Ryan was at the grocery store, and I felt a nervous breakdown coming on, so I decided once more to go to God with my questions and overwhelming emotions. Then I heard as clear as day: *These are not your children.*

I burst into tears. God continued to minister to me as He reminded me that He loved Blair, Barrett, and Blake more than I did and that "no purpose of [God's] can be thwarted" (Job 42:2). I had never been in control, I still was not in control, and ultimately I didn't want to be in control—because God was the One who knew what needed to happen. And He had promised to help me every step of the way.

This lesson saw me through the longest hours and the darkest nights. As Matthew 16:25 says, "Whoever wishes to save his life will lose it, but whoever loses his life for My sake will find it." Losing my control allowed me to find my faith. The freedom found in letting God be responsible provides the peace we need in order to pray big things.

Persistence in Prayer

The Merriam-Webster Learner's Dictionary defines *persistence* as "the quality that allows someone to continue doing something or trying to do something even though it is difficult or opposed by other people."[1] We are often too lazy about prayer, too flippant, too distracted, too unwilling to look at biblical guidelines for the spiritual discipline that allows us to approach the throne of grace with confidence so that we may find help in our time of need.

After nine years of student ministry, the same awkward chirping of cricket sounds still happens when I ask a group of teenagers who wants to pray at the end of a Bible study. We often have no trouble talking to everyone else about our issues, problems, desires, challenges, and hopes, but for some reason we rarely if ever have that conversation with the One who is able to actually change our situations. How much energy are we wasting? How many blessings are we missing?

The Bible is clear that it is possible for Christians to miss out on things God has for us. I don't want to get to heaven and see what could have been mine if only I had asked. Isaiah 30:18 explains God's desire to help us: "The LORD longs to be gracious to you; therefore he will rise up to show you compassion. For the LORD is a God of justice. Blessed are all who wait for him!" (NIV). He is not an unrighteous judge but a perfect God, and in Him there is no evil.

> *It is possible for Christians to miss out on things God has for us.*

Our Struggle Is Not against Flesh and Blood

"The LORD is a warrior; the LORD is His name" (Exod. 15:3). I remember giving this verse to a friend of mine who had just had her world rocked by the news her husband wanted a divorce. In the blink of an eye, her world was turned upside down and her faith was tested like never before. She did not know what to do. From the looks of things, he had outsmarted her, outlawyered her, and outwitted her. She was blindsided, and he was prepared.

Distraught and devastated, my friend who had been under her husband's covering in an instant became solely reliant on God's covering. I remember getting up in the middle of the night because the Holy Spirit led me to text her Exodus 14:14: "The LORD will fight for you; you need only to be still" (NIV). She went through many months of emotions, prayers, unveiled secrets, and tests of faith.

I remember one day when my friend came over in particularly high spirits. I inquired about her new demeanor, and she said, "I'm just really excited because I stayed up all night watching kidnapping documentaries."

"I'm sorry, I think I missed something. Um, what?"

She replied, "I know that sounds weird, but I figured out there is one main component for families that find justice for their children and ones that don't. The families that find their children and find out the truth refuse to give up. And I'm just not going to give up." (Yes, of course, there are also parents who have fought with all their being to find their children and bring their captors to justice without ever being able to do so.)

In the midst of marriages ending, children choosing wrong paths, or loss of jobs, relationships, or position, it is easy to decide this world and the people in it are the problem. We think, *If only they would change, if only this would change, if only my situation would change,* then *everything would be okay.* But Ephesians 6:12 stops us in our tracks like a deer frozen in headlights: "For our struggle is not against flesh and blood, but against the rulers, against the authorities, against the powers of this dark world and against the spiritual forces of evil in the heavenly realms" (NIV). And James reminds us, "Resist the devil and he will flee from you" (James 4:7).

When we find ourselves in times of spiritual warfare, we must remember the spiritual power we have in the name of Jesus. Ephesians 1:21–23 reminds us that Jesus is "far above all rule and authority and power and dominion, and every name that is named, not only in this age but also in the one to come. And He put all things in subjection under His feet, and gave Him as head over all things to the church, which is His body, the fullness of Him who fills all in all."

While people have all kinds of philosophies, mantras, life verses, and motivational sayings, the simple decision to not give up ensures our life will look different from that of those who do. Persistence is key to defeating our enemy. Satan lurks in the corner, hissing to us in the middle of marriage arguments, in times of intense depression and despair, in times of questioning God's goodness, "Give up . . . Give up . . . Give up . . ." We must choose to persist in prayer and fight temptation with all we can—and then we can rest in the fact that God fights for us always, even when we have nothing left.

> *Persistence is key to defeating our enemy.*

Living with Our Hands Open

Never giving up means we keep inviting that non-Christian family member to church even after years of awkward rejections. Never giving up means our children are always welcomed back home regardless of what they have or haven't done. Never giving up means we see the doctors whom we are supposed to see in order to serve God to the best of our ability in the healthiest body possible. Never giving up means we fight for our marriages, our churches, our faith, our country, and our family. Never giving up means we leave nothing behind and are able to stand before Christ on the day we meet Him face-to-face, honestly and humbly bow before Him, and say, "I gave it my all, Lord."

There is a balance between fighting with all we have and releasing to God what is beyond our control. As the well-known Serenity Prayer says, "God, grant me the serenity to accept the things I cannot change, courage to change the things I can, and wisdom to know the difference." While thousands of those who have received help from twelve-step programs can rattle off this prayer in their sleep, let's take a look at the lesser known second stanza of this prayer by theologian Reinhold Niebuhr:

> Living one day at a time,
> Enjoying one moment at a time,
> Accepting hardships as the pathway to peace;
> Taking, as He did, this sinful world
> As it is, not as I would have it;
> Trusting that He will make all things right
> If I surrender to His Will;
> So that I may be reasonably happy in this life
> And supremely happy with Him
> Forever and ever in the next.
> Amen.[2]

This is a stark contrast to the phrase, "It is what it is." God does not want us to adopt a hands-off approach to life but rather a hands-open approach to life. When we live with our hands open, we understand all we have is from God, and He has a right to all of us and all we have. This is not fear but freedom.

Joseph—An Example of Persistence

Joseph kept going. Even though he was abandoned by his brothers, sold into slavery, wrongly accused, thrown into prison, and forgotten by people who promised to help him, he never gave up and never took time off from furthering the cause of the God he trusted. Joseph is a great example of someone who refused to give up. Despite his circumstances, in the face of his enemies, in the isolation of his imprisonment, he kept going and God kept blessing. He had so many opportunities to decide God was not for him and he therefore needed to go at it alone or give up entirely. The main principle found in Joseph's life could be summed up in three words: "He kept going." Often the simplest decision to not give in or give up will be the defining decision that changes your life.

Choose Your Mindset

As Captain Jack Sparrow wisely said, "The problem is not the problem. The problem is your attitude about the problem."[3] Perhaps one of the greatest fatalities of Christianity is that Jesus's followers have been convinced they should never suffer, and that if they do suffer something is wrong and their faith is void. Suffering actually means we are doing something right and that we are now in the game.

Being called to suffer is often the result of being a sold-out Christian. Picture an athlete sitting on the bench pleading, "Put me in, Coach! Put me in!" In their book *The Way Back*, Phil Cooke and Jonathan Bock describe the radical commitment to Jesus that many first-century Christians in the Roman Empire had despite horrific persecution and certain death.

> The "Super Bowl" of the time in Rome was the Coliseum—a place where human beings were ripped apart and devoured by wild animals for the amusement of the general public. . . .
>
> The goal of these public tortures and murders was to snuff out this potentially dangerous cult and discourage others from joining. Roman authorities assumed public shaming and executions would put a stop to what they considered to be foolishness about this Jewish teacher named Jesus.
>
> To make the necessary example, the church fathers were typically chosen first. But to the surprise of the Roman authorities, the line of the willing grew. Once a bishop was murdered, a priest would step forward. Once that priest was executed, a local deacon would volunteer. Behind that deacon stood a line that never ended of believers ready to meet their death rather than recant or denounce the name of Jesus.
>
> In fact, the numbers were so great that church fathers were forced to forbid voluntary martyrdom. But in spite of those well-meaning decrees, surviving documents report a very large number of men and women who still *volunteered* to be martyrs for their faith.
>
> Through it all, these early believers held fast. Their remarkable and unrelenting commitment to the faith gave

Christianity a credibility that transformed their perception in the eyes of the Romans.[4]

History reveals that the impact these Christian martyrs had on the Romans was powerful and compelling. Cooke and Bock conclude, "Rome was certainly the most powerful empire on the planet, but when it came to unwavering commitment, the Roman authorities had met their match."[5]

Pursue Peace

We cannot always live in a fight-or-flight mindset and, thankfully, we are not supposed to. If the Bible shows us anything about the pattern of battles, it is that there are seasons of training and battles but also seasons of refreshing. We have to learn to distinguish between them.

Jesus didn't exactly need training, but He was baptized by John the Baptist in a time of obeying and submitting to God's command before taking Satan on literally face-to-face. Almost immediately after His baptism, Jesus was tested in the wilderness for forty days and forty nights by the prince of darkness. In perhaps the biggest battle of His earthly life, Jesus used Scripture to fight the lies being thrown at him like flaming arrows by the father of lies. After this intense time of testing, Jesus experienced a time of incredible encouragement as He began His ministry, called the disciples, and spent three years completely changing the world with the fulfillment of the gospel.

What assurance and comfort to know that while Jesus will ultimately win the war on darkness in the end times, He also was able to win against Satan in His personal life by clinging to Scripture. Pursuing peaceful lives, allowing ourselves to rest, and spending time with people who are spiritually refreshing to us allows us the energy to fight when it is time to do battle and the energy to say, "Get behind me, Satan!" (Matt. 16:23).

Never Give In

"Success is going from one failure to another without loss of enthusiasm," Winston Churchill reportedly said. However, success is not our ultimate goal as Christians. Finishing well and hearing "Well done, good and faithful servant!" is our ultimate prize (Matt. 25:21 NIV). We should never romanticize suffering or persecution, but its presence should not come as a surprise as part of God's plan for our lives.

> *We should never romanticize suffering or persecution, but its presence should not come as a surprise as part of God's plan for our lives.*

Being a good and faithful servant is going from one trial to the next without taking our eyes off of Jesus, "the author and perfecter of faith" (Heb. 12:2). We may limp, and we may need a fellow soldier to carry us at times, but at the end of the day we know the war we are fighting—and we refuse to give up.

On October 29, 1941, in the midst of World War II, Winston Churchill gave a now-famous inspirational speech at his alma mater, Harrow School, that emphasizes the choice we have in keeping our enemy in perspective: "Never give in, never give in, never, never, never, never—in nothing, great or small, large or petty—never give in except to convictions of honour and good sense. Never yield to force;

179

never yield to the apparently overwhelming might of the enemy."[6]

The attacks of our enemy can feel overwhelming, but Jesus reminds us, "Take courage; I have overcome the world" (John 16:33).

Take Action

What strategy can we use to persevere in prayer despite the attacks of the enemy of our souls? The invincible combination of naming our enemy, recognizing our power, and choosing not to give up is the winning tactic for all of life's battles.

Name Our Enemy

It's impossible to fight an enemy we have not named. One of Satan's biggest tricks is painting other people, outside problems, and even God as our problem. Satan used this tactic in the garden when he tempted Eve into believing God was withholding something good from her. "You surely will not die! For God knows that in the day you eat from it your eyes will be opened, and you will be like God, knowing good and evil" (Gen. 3:5). Satan is still trying to confuse us about who our real enemy is, but Ephesians 6:12 makes it resoundingly clear that our struggle is "against the spiritual forces of evil in the heavenly realms" (NIV). When we pray, we go to battle. Praying gets God's attention, yes, but it also gets Satan's attention.

> *Prayer is more than a nice family tradition. Prayer is a matter of life and death.*

"Does Satan know your name?" my student minister often asked us while I was in his ministry. The idea is that if we are really going to start living for Christ, preaching the gospel to others, and doing everything in our power to bring as many people as possible to heaven, we need to realize we have set ourselves against the darkest forces in this world, and there is an X on our back. Does this mean we stop? No. Does this mean we give in? Never. Realizing Satan knows our names when we go into prayer battling for others, for our marriages, and for our ministries helps each of us understand that prayer is more than a nice family tradition. Prayer is a matter of life and death.

Naming our enemy is not meant to create fear but to help us prepare for battle. We know who wins in the end. If we are followers of Christ, we are on the winning side.

Recognize Our Power

I was hesitant to write a book on prayer. Others often seem to be books about theological theories on the spiritual discipline and stories of nineteenth-century preachers exercising old world prayer disciplines that maybe we should consider implementing in the twenty-first century. I just don't have a lot to say about any of that. But what I do know is that in my time of praying big things, I unlocked a power I never knew before and it changed my life, my family, and my world forever.

Looking back, the main change I made was taking God at His Word. I claimed the promise of James 4:2–3, which says, "You do not have because you do not ask God. When you ask, you do not receive, because you ask with wrong motives, that you may spend what you get on your pleasures" (NIV).

And I reminded God of His promise in Ephesians 3:20–21, which tells us, "Now to him who is able to do immeasurably more than all we ask or imagine, according to his power that is at work within us, to him be glory in the church and in Christ Jesus throughout all generations, for ever and ever! Amen" (NIV). Then I stood on my tiptoes and grasped like a little kid in a candy store at all the possibilities those prayers opened for me.

Praying God's literal words helps us to be on the same page with God, using the same language with the same motives, hearts, dreams, and powers. We do not always have to pray only using Scripture, but it is a good place to start. Praying God's Word allows us to know we are praying God's will. And God answers the prayers that align with His will.

Praying God's Word allows us to know we are praying God's will.

The best way to know God's will is to read Scripture. Praying Scripture aligns our words with God's perfect will, creating a new power behind our requests. The Bible says,

> Praise be to the God and Father of our Lord Jesus Christ! In his great mercy he has given us new birth into a living hope through the resurrection of Jesus Christ from the dead, and into an inheritance that can never perish, spoil or fade. This inheritance is kept in heaven for you, who through faith are shielded by God's power until the coming of the salvation that is ready to be revealed in the last time. (1 Pet. 1:3–5 NIV)

Combine this truth with the power God says is available to us in Ephesians 1:19–20: "I also pray that you will understand the incredible greatness of God's power for us who believe him. This is the same mighty power that raised Christ from the dead and seated him in the place of honor at God's right hand in the heavenly realms" (NLT).

We have an imperishable inheritance and an invincible power that Satan is hoping we never tap into but is waiting, wanting, and ready to be unleashed. This power is more fantastic than Pandora's box and more adventure-filled than the wardrobe to Narnia. This power is your destiny waiting to be claimed.

Decide to Never Give Up

The only way to lose is to quit. We do not have to win at being the best parent, best spouse, or best anything. This is something Jesus frees us from pursuing because He lets us know that He is the only perfect One, and we will not be perfect until we go to heaven.

> *The only way to lose is to quit.*

I remember our last night in the hospital. I woke up about a thousand times with the realization that I had just had three babies come out of my tummy. During one of these middle-of-the-night awakenings, I had a wonderful going-home present from God as I woke up to see my faithful husband sleeping on the couch next to me like he had slept for the past forty-nine days in the hospital. But this time he was smiling and had one arm totally extended in the air. I watched in confusion, then I began to smile too, since he was clearly so happy in his dream.

The next morning, I told him what I had seen. He replied, "Oh, that must be because I was dreaming that I was praising God in a worship service!"

Ryan was the living example of Psalm 63:6: "I remember You on my bed, I meditate on You in the night watches." We don't become inclined to praise God in our sleep without first going through the fire. We get this kind of intimacy in worship by facing our problems, our doubts, and the struggles that seem to threaten our very existence. We get it by choosing never to give up. We wake up daily, our eyes fixed on Jesus, with the resolve, "Though He slay me, I will hope in Him" (Job 13:15).

We Know How the Story Ends

I heard a comedian one time talking about his experience while watching the Mel Gibson film *The Passion of the Christ*. His stand-up routine included reenacting the looks he was getting while talking during the film. One lady repeatedly kept shushing him until finally he shot back, "Hey! I know how the story ends!" I can't recall the comedian's motivation in telling this story, but that line has remained with me ever since. No matter what we see happening in our lives, our families, our work, or our world, we know how the story ends. Jesus wins. He said, "If I go and prepare a place for you, I will come again and receive you to Myself, that where I am, there you may be also" (John 14:3). Jesus is coming back!

Because of Christ, we have the power even in the midst of defeat to persevere and to keep praying big things.

There is an ultimate war to be won, but until that day comes, God has given us the power to win every battle leading up to it. Difficult times remind us that this world is not a playground but a battleground that demands we pray big things. We are not alone when we're tempted to give up or give in. Because of Christ, we have the power even in the midst of defeat to persevere and to keep praying big things.

Conclusion

When God Gives You Everything You Want and More

I really hope we can be featured on a TV show!" I exclaimed to Ryan the day we found out we were having triplets. "People need to hear that God answers prayer." What could be dismissed as a millennial pipe dream turned out to be a God-ordained dream. I didn't want to be on a TV show to help pay for the formula and thousands of diapers we go through each day (trust me, reality TV is not something you do for money!). I wanted to do it to have the opportunity to share God's story of faithfulness to the biggest audience possible. After learning we were pregnant with the triplets, we were clearly on a kick for praying big things and, at this point, nothing seemed too big for God. We began praying that God would allow our miracle story to be broadcasted on television, and four months later TLC called asking us to share our story on their show *Rattled*.

God will give you everything you want when everything you want is Him. He is able to use the prayers, the plans, and the dreams that we often think originated with us and not only fulfill them but also turn them into great stories of His faithfulness, love, and power. God can be trusted to give us our hearts' desires, but we must want Him more than for what He can give us.

When God gives us the big things we have prayed for, our next step is to get to work honoring God with these gifts, remembering God's goodness, and proclaiming His faithfulness.

> *God will give you everything you want when everything you want is Him.*

I remember the TV show showrunner asking me in the middle of one of our filming days if I had ever doubted my faith during our struggle with miscarriages, the high-risk pregnancy, and the hospital stays. The answer was simple. No. I told the showrunner that there was no security in doubting God or in trying to live this journey without Him, so I had decided to take God at His Word. I'm not talking about a mere humming of the childhood song "Jesus loves me, this I know" (though sometimes that is all our pained hearts can muster). I'm talking about the days I spent quoting and claiming Scripture as I never had before.

I remember, morning after morning on hospital bedrest, asking the nurses not to come into my room so I could spend time with God on my hospital bed crying out to Him, "To You, O LORD, I called, and to the Lord I made supplication: 'What profit is there in my blood, if I go down to the pit? Will the dust praise You? Will it declare Your faithfulness?'" (Ps. 30:8–9). I remember telling God time and again, "I know You are good no matter what happens, and I will follow You no matter what happens, but I beg You to save my children, because I have been faithful to You and so many believers are praying to You. We need this win."

This was in no way intended to boss God around—far from it! I was merely following the example of the psalmist who made this same case in his prayers to God. If we all died, there would be no praise coming from me or my children because we wouldn't be around to declare God's faithfulness.

The lifestyle of praying big things includes telling anyone and everyone of the big things God has done in our life. Acts 4:20 says, "We cannot stop speaking about what we have seen and heard," and it has become a life verse for our family after our miracle journey. It's our privilege and our responsibility to tell others about God's work in our lives so they can be encouraged to trust Him to work in their lives.

Psalm 37:4 says, "Delight yourself in the LORD; and He will give you the desires of your heart." The order of this well-known Bible verse is so important. We first must delight, love, seek, and run after Jesus. After our story aired on *Rattled*, I received thousands of messages on social media from people around the world, thanking me for being a "positive light on television for Christ," for "giving them hope to keep asking God for children," and for "showing it's possible to trust God even in loss and fear." These comments and others like them remind me of the importance of telling others about the work God does in our lives.

We gain an incredible energy and excitement from hearing how God has powerfully moved in other people's lives. Testimonies of God's faithfulness remind us of the goodness and power of the God we serve and give us courage to face our battles with even more faith and ferocity. "Is anything too difficult for the LORD?" (Gen. 18:14) needs to be the promise with which we face every challenge, every dream, every prayer.

Nothing is too difficult for the Lord, and He loves proving so.

> *Nothing is too difficult for the Lord, and He loves proving so.*

This period of miscarriages, infertility, triplet pregnancy, bedrest, and babies in the NICU allowed us an opportunity for the rubber to meet the road. It enabled me to see firsthand the fulfillment of promises of Scripture that I had memorized as a child. Back then, these verses were a homework assignment. But as an adult, they were my lifeline and the only hope available as I lay in a hospital bed wondering if I would live and if my children would live. You never know God is all you need until God is all you have.

Don't Let Anyone Rob Your Joy

It's been unbelievable how much Satan has tried to rob the joy, the specialness, and the miracle of our story. The most common way he has used people to discourage us is when we share our story of praying for multiples, for three biological children, and for "God to do more than anything we could hope or imagine," and someone remarks, "Yeah, but you used fertility drugs, right?" Like air slowly being let out of a balloon that had been soaring toward the open sky, our story suddenly loses air and falls to the ground. Then I remember that our story is God's story, and Satan has been trying to take away from God's story and glory from the beginning of time.

Want God More Than Anything Else on Earth

Wanting God more than anything this world has to offer does not happen by default. It is a mindset and a lifestyle that must be fought for.

I was disappointed when I found out that TLC chose not to have us on the premiere of the show. After months of filming, that was the production company's decision. We were in every episode except one after that, but it still was a tough blow. I asked God to help me see the situation as He did. In His strength I was able to thank Him for the fact that even though we hadn't made the premiere, another Christian couple was going to be featured, and in the end that is what mattered—not that our story was featured but that God's message was shared.

This was a humbling lesson and an important opportunity to remember there are only two teams, two sides, two armies in this world: God's and the enemy's. We have to want Jesus more than anything else in this world—more than health, more than opportunities, more than fame, more than a family, more than anything.

What Big Prayer Do You Have?

"Although the world is full of suffering, it is full also of the overcoming of it," Helen Keller once said.[1] People need to hear our stories. They need to hear that God is real, He is active, and He is good. It is our job not merely to tell our story but to tell of His story in our lives.

Colossians 4:5 commands us to be wise with the opportunities God gives us: "Conduct yourselves with wisdom toward outsiders, *making the most of the opportunity*." I urge you to make the most out of every opportunity you have to share the gospel and your story with others. God has given you a story, and God has given you people with whom to share your story.

As for us, Ryan and I truly believe the triplets are a miraculous answer to our specific and persistent prayers. The triplets are not our story—they belong to a God who is able and who did more than we could imagine!

What big prayer do you want to start asking God today?

While triplets are rare, the true rarity is not in God's answering big prayers but in our *asking* big prayers. What big prayer do you want to start asking God today? God is waiting, listening, and daring you to pray big things!

Notes

Chapter 1 More Than We Can Imagine

1. Barna Group, "Six Reasons Young Christians Leave the Church," Barna .com, September 27, 2011, https://www.barna.com/research/six-reasons-young -christians-leave-church/.

2. C. S. Lewis, *Mere Christianity*, rev. and exp. ed. (New York: HarperOne, 2015), 50.

3. Mark Batterson, *Draw the Circle* (Grand Rapids: Zondervan, 2012), 25.

Chapter 2 Is Anybody Up There?

1. A. W. Tozer, *The Knowledge of the Holy* (New York: HarperCollins, 1961), 1.

2. Barna Group, "Two-Thirds of Christians Face Doubt," Barna.com, July 25, 2017, https://www.barna.com/research/two-thirds-christians-face-doubt/.

3. Barna Group, "Two-Thirds of Christians Face Doubt."

4. Although the source of this quote is uncertain, it is often attributed to President Calvin Coolidge in 1929. An earlier version appeared in Theodore T. Munger, *On the Threshold* (Boston: Houghton, Mifflin and Co., 1880), 9.

5. F. B. Meyer, *Abraham or the Obedience of Faith* (Grand Rapids: Zondervan, 1954), 148.

6. Warren Wiersbe, *Be Patient (Job): Waiting on God in Difficult Times* (Colorado Springs: David C. Cook, 2009), 117, emphasis in original.

Chapter 3 Work Hard, Pray Harder

1. "1848: John Quincy Adams Suffers a Stroke," *This Day in History*, February 21, https://www.history.com/this-day-in-history/john-quincy-adams-suffers-a-stroke.

2. Robert Samuelson, "How John Quincy Adams Made Lincoln Possible," *The Weekly Standard*, July 11, 2017, https://www.weeklystandard.com/richard -samuelson/how-john-quincy-adams-made-lincoln-possible.

3. John Bradshaw, *Healing the Shame That Binds You* (Deerfield Beach, FL: Health Communications, Inc., 2005), 46.

4. C. S. Lewis, *The Lion, the Witch and the Wardrobe* (New York: HarperCollins, 2008), 79.

5. Christine Caine, *Undaunted: Daring to Do What God Calls You to Do* (Grand Rapids: Zondervan, 2012), 170.

6. Elisabeth Elliot, speech at Urbana '79, as quoted by Gordon Govier, "Elisabeth Elliot," Urbana.org, June 16, 2005, https://urbana.org/blog/elisabeth-elliot.

Chapter 4 Don't Just Pray

1. "Spider-Man (2002) Quotes," IMDB, accessed March 8, 2019, https://www.imdb.com/title/tt0145487/.

2. Merriam-Webster Online Dictionary, s.v. common sense, accessed January 16, 2019, https://www.merriam-webster.com/dictionary/common%20sense.

Chapter 5 When God Says Yes

1. Mark Batterson, *Draw the Circle* (Grand Rapids: Zondervan, 2012).

Chapter 6 Panic and Prayer Warriors

1. Curt Thompson, *Anatomy of the Soul: Surprising Connections between Neuroscience and Spiritual Practices That Can Transform Your Life and Relationships*, 3rd ed. (Carol Stream, IL: Tyndale Momentum, 2010).

2. David Benner, *The Gift of Being Yourself: The Sacred Call to Self-Discovery* (Downers Grove, IL: InterVarsity Press, 2015), 54.

3. Corrie ten Boom, *Each New Day: 365 Reflections to Strengthen Your Faith* (Grand Rapids: Revell, 2003), 61.

Chapter 7 Purpose in the Pain

1. William Ernest Henley, "Invictus," *A Book of Verses* (London: D. Nutt, 1888), 56–57.

2. Joni Eareckson Tada, "My Testimony," *Joni and Friends*, January 27, 2014, http://www.nohio.joniandfriends.org/radio/4-minute/my-testimony/.

3. Joni Eareckson Tada, "Reflections on the 50th Anniversary of My Diving Accident," The Gospel Coalition, July 30, 2017, https://www.thegospelcoalition.org/article/reflections-on-50th-anniversary-of-my-diving-accident/.

4. John Bradshaw, *Healing the Shame That Binds You* (Deerfield Beach, FL: Health Communications, Inc., 2005), 46.

Chapter 8 Unanswered Prayers

1. C. S. Lewis, *A Grief Observed* (New York: HarperOne, 2001), 52.

2. Heidi Murkoff, "Your Tentative Timetable," *What to Expect*, February 27, 2015, https://www.whattoexpect.com/pregnancy/twins-and-multiples/giving-birth/your-tentative-timetable.aspx.

3. James Emery White, "Thankful for the Fleas," Crosswalk.com, accessed January 21, 2019, https://www.crosswalk.com/print/11660743/.

Chapter 9 Dream Big, Give Thanks, and Have Fun

1. "This Is Your Brain on Fun: The Science behind Learning, Motivation, and Having a Great Time," *Kites in the Classroom*, July 21, 2018, https://kitesinthe classroom.com/your-brain-on-fun/.

2. *Ever After: A Cinderella Story*, directed by Andy Tennant, written by Susannah Grant and Rick Parks (Los Angeles: Twentieth Century Fox), released July 31, 1998.

3. The exact origin of this quote is unknown.

4. Richard Florida, "The Unhappy States of America," *City Lab*, March 20, 2018, https://www.citylab.com/life/2018/03/the-unhappy-states-of-america/555800/.

5. Kate Bratskeir, "21 Percent of Americans Are Online Basically All the Time," *Huffington Post*, December 9, 2015, https://www.huffingtonpost.com/entry /american-time-spent-online-is-outrageous_us_566863cfe4b080eddf567867.

Chapter 10 Never Give Up

1. Merriam-Webster Learner's Dictionary, s.v. persistence, accessed January 22, 2019, http://www.learnersdictionary.com/definition/persistence.

2. Reinhold Niebuhr, "Serenity Prayer" (1943), public domain.

3. "The 15 Most Important *Pirates of the Caribbean* Quotes, According to You," *Oh My Disney*, accessed January 22, 2019, https://ohmy.disney.com/movies /2016/01/05/the-15-most-important-pirates-of-the-caribbean-quotes-according -to-you/.

4. Phil Cooke and Jonathan Bock, *The Way Back: How Christians Blew Our Credibility and How We Get It Back* (Nashville: Worthy, 2018), 62–64.

5. Cooke and Bock, *The Way Back*, 64.

6. Winston Churchill, "Never Give In, Never, Never, Never, 1941," speech at Harrow School, October 29, 1941, https://www.nationalchurchillmuseum.org /never-give-in-never-never-never.html.

Conclusion

1. Helen Keller, *Optimism* (1903; repr. Scotts Valley, CA: CreateSpace Independent Publishing Platform, 2018), 8.

About the Author

Julia Jeffress Sadler is a reality star from TLC's *Rattled* who has seen God do immeasurably more than anything she could hope or imagine. After they suffered three miscarriages in one year, God blessed her and her husband, Ryan, with triplets. Their story of faith, prayer, and evangelism in the midst of heartache has encouraged thousands around the world.

Julia is a licensed professional counselor and the girls ministry director at the thirteen-thousand-member First Baptist Church of Dallas, Texas. She trained at the world-renowned Meier Clinics, where she specialized in treating teenagers and adults struggling with depression, anxiety, and eating disorders. Julia is a regular conference speaker, radio show guest, and host of *The Julia Sadler Show*.

Her clinical training, biblical foundation, pastor's daughter upbringing, and sense of humor provide a fresh perspective on cultural topics. Julia and her junior-high sweetheart, Ryan, live and minister in Dallas, Texas. Connect with Julia at juliajsadler.com!

YOU CAN BOOK
Julia!

women | college students | teens | moms

Julia loves speaking to hundreds of teenagers weekly at
First Baptist Dallas and to thousands of viewers through
The Julia Sadler Show. Julia also speaks at women's conferences
and college campuses around the country on the following topics:

Rattled: TV Show, Triplets & Trusting God along the Way

Pray Big Things: Discovering the Life You Were Meant to Live

More Than Anything We Can Imagine: Infertility & Triplet Testimony

Tell the World: Evangelism Training & Encouragement

Living a Legacy: Making the Most out of Your Life Today

Real Talk: What the Bible Says about Depression, Self-Harm, Anxiety & Suicide

Sugar: God's Sweet Plan for Purity & Dating

Worth More: Eating Disorders & Identity

From Ruined to Redeemed: Why It's Never Too Late to Follow God

juliajsadler.com

Connect
with
Julia!

juliajsadler.com

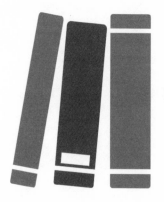

LIKE THIS
BOOK?
Consider sharing it with others!

- Share or mention the book on your social media platforms. Use the hashtag **#PrayBigThings**.

- Write a book review on your blog or on a retailer site.

- Pick up a copy for friends, family, or anyone who you think would enjoy and be challenged by its message!

- Share this message on Twitter **@juliajsadler**, Facebook **@juliasadler: thesadlertriplets**, or Instagram **@juliajsadler_thesadlertriplets**: I loved **#PrayBigThings** // **@ReadBakerBooks**

- Recommend this book for your church, workplace, book club, or class.

- Follow Baker Books on social media and tell us what you like.

 **ReadBakerBooks**

 **ReadBakerBooks**

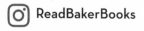 **ReadBakerBooks**